Higher Lessons in English

A Work on English Grammar

Brainerd Kellogg

PREFACE.

The plan of "Higher Lessons" will perhaps be better understood if we first speak of two classes of text-books with which this work is brought into competition.

+Method of One Class of Text-books+.—In one class are those that aim chiefly to present a course of technical grammar in the order of Orthography, Etymology, Syntax, and Prosody. These books give large space to grammatical Etymology, and demand much memorizing of definitions, rules, declensions, and conjugations, and much formal word parsing,—work of which a considerable portion is merely the invention of grammarians, and has little value in determining the pupil's use of language or in developing his reasoning faculties. This is a revival of the long-endured, unfruitful, old-time method.

+Method of Another Class of Text-books.+—In another class are those that present a miscellaneous collection of lessons in Composition, Spelling, Pronunciation, Sentence-analysis, Technical Grammar, and General Information, without unity or continuity. The pupil who completes these books will have gained something by practice and will have picked up some scraps of knowledge; but his information will be vague and disconnected, and he will have missed that mental training which it is the aim of a good text-book to afford. A text-book is of value just so far as it presents a clear, logical development of its subject. It must present its science or its art as a natural growth, otherwise there is no apology for its being.

+The Study of the Sentence for the Proper Use of Words.+—It is the plan of *this* book to trace with easy steps the natural development of the sentence, to consider the leading facts first and then to descend to the details. To begin with the parts of speech is to begin with details and to disregard the higher unities, without which the details are scarcely intelligible. The part of speech to which a word belongs is determined only by its function in the sentence, and inflections simply mark the offices and relations of words. Unless the pupil has been systematically trained to discover the functions and relations of words as elements of an organic whole, his knowledge of the parts of speech is of little value. It is not because he cannot conjugate the verb or decline the pronoun that he falls into such errors as "How many sounds *have* each of the vowels?" "Five years' interest *are* due." "She is older than *me*." He probably would not say "each *have*," "interest *are*," "*me* am." One thoroughly familiar with the structure of the sentence will find little trouble in using correctly the few inflectional forms in English.

+The Study of the Sentence for the Laws of Discourse.+—Through the study of the sentence we not only arrive at an intelligent knowledge of the parts of speech and a correct use of grammatical forms, but we discover the laws of discourse in general. In the sentence the student should find the law of unity, of continuity, of proportion, of order. All good writing consists of good sentences properly joined. Since the sentence is the foundation or unit of discourse, it is all-important that the pupil should know the sentence. He should be able to put the principal and the subordinate parts in their proper relation; he should know the exact function of every element, its relation to other elements and its relation to the whole. He should know the sentence as the skillful engineer knows his engine, that, when there is a disorganization of parts, he may at once find the difficulty and the remedy for it.

+The Study of the Sentence for the Sake of Translation.+—The laws of thought being the same for all nations, the logical analysis of the sentence is the same for all languages. When a student who has acquired a knowledge of the English sentence comes to the translation of a foreign language, he finds his work greatly simplified. If in a sentence of his own language he sees only a mass of unorganized words, how much greater must be his confusion when this mass of words is in a foreign tongue! A study of the parts of speech is a far less important preparation for translation, since the declensions and conjugations in English do not conform to those of other languages. Teachers of the classics and of modern languages are beginning to appreciate these facts.

+The Study of the Sentence for Discipline+.—As a means of discipline nothing can compare with a training in the logical analysis of the sentence. To study thought through its outward form, the sentence, and to discover the fitness of the different parts of the expression to the parts of the thought, is to learn to think. It has been noticed that pupils thoroughly trained in the analysis and the construction of sentences come to their other studies with a decided advantage in mental power. These results can be obtained only by systematic and persistent work. Experienced teachers understand that a few weak lessons on the sentence at the beginning of a course and a few at the end can afford little discipline and little knowledge that will endure, nor can a knowledge of the sentence be gained by memorizing complicated rules and labored forms of analysis. To compel a pupil to wade through a page or two of such bewildering terms as "complex adverbial element of the second class" and "compound prepositional adjective phrase," in order to comprehend a few simple functions, is grossly unjust; it is a substitution of form for content, of words for ideas.

+Subdivisions and Modifications after the Sentence.+—Teachers familiar with text-books that group all grammatical instruction around the eight parts of speech, making eight independent units, will not, in the following lessons, find everything in its accustomed place. But, when it is remembered that the thread of connection unifying this work is the sentence, it will be seen that the lessons fall into their natural order of sequence. When, through the development of the sentence, all the offices of the different parts of speech are mastered, the most natural thing is to continue the work of classification and subdivide the parts of speech. The inflection of words, being distinct from their classification, makes a separate division of the work. If the chief end of grammar were to enable one to parse, we should not here depart from long-established precedent.

+Sentences in Groups—Paragraphs+.—In tracing the growth of the sentence from the simplest to the most complex form, each element, as it is introduced, is illustrated by a large number of detached sentences, chosen with the utmost care as to thought and expression. These compel the pupil to confine his attention to one thing till he gets it well in hand. Paragraphs from literature are then selected to be used at intervals, with questions and suggestions to enforce principles already presented, and to prepare the way informally for the regular lessons that follow. The lessons on these selections are, however, made to take a much wider scope. They lead the pupil to discover how and why sentences are grouped into paragraphs, and how paragraphs are related to each other; they also lead him on to discover whatever is most worthy of imitation in the style of the several models presented.

+The Use of the Diagram+.—In written analysis, the simple map, or diagram, found in the following lessons, will enable the pupil to present directly and vividly to the eye the exact function of every clause in the sentence, of every phrase in the clause, and of every word in the phrase—to picture the complete analysis of the sentence, with principal and subordinate parts in their proper relations. It is only by the aid of such a map, or picture, that the pupil can, at a single view, see the sentence as an organic whole made up of many parts performing various functions and standing in various relations. Without such map he must labor under the disadvantage of seeing all these things by piecemeal or in succession.

But if for any reason the teacher prefers not to use these diagrams, they may be omitted without causing the slightest break in the work. The plan of this book is in no way dependent on the use of the diagrams.

+The Objections to the Diagram+.—The fact that the pictorial diagram groups the parts of a sentence according to their offices and relations, and not in the order of speech, has been spoken of as a fault. It is, on the contrary, a merit, for it teaches the pupil to look through the literary order and discover the logical order. He thus learns what the literary order really is, and sees that this may be varied indefinitely, so long as the logical relations are kept clear.

The assertion that correct diagrams can be made mechanically is not borne out by the facts. It is easier to avoid precision in oral analysis than in written. The diagram drives the pupil to a most searching examination of the sentence, brings him face to face with every difficulty, and compels a decision on every point.

+The Abuse of the Diagram+.—Analysis by diagram often becomes so interesting and so helpful that, like other good things, it is liable to be overdone. There is danger of requiring too much written analysis. When the ordinary constructions have been made clear, diagrams should be used only for the more difficult sentences, or, if the sentences are long, only for the more difficult parts of them. In both oral and written analysis there is danger of repeating what needs no repetition. When the diagram has served its purpose, it should be dropped.

AUTHORS' NOTE TO REVISED EDITION.

During the years in which "Higher Lessons" has been in existence, we have ourselves had an instructive experience with it in the classroom. We have considered hundreds of suggestive letters written us by intelligent teachers using the book. We have examined the best works on grammar that have been published recently here and in England. And we have done more. We have gone to the original source of all valid authority in our language— the best writers and speakers of it. That we might ascertain what present linguistic usage is, we chose fifty authors, now alive or living till recently, and have carefully read three hundred pages of each. We have minutely noted and recorded what these men by habitual use declare to be good English. Among the fifty are such men as Ruskin, Froude, Hamerton, Matthew Arnold, Macaulay, De Quincey, Thackeray, Bagehot, John Morley, James Martineau, Cardinal Newman, J. R. Green, and Lecky in England; and Hawthorne, Curtis, Prof. W. D. Whitney, George P. Marsh, Prescott, Emerson, Motley, Prof. Austin Phelps, Holmes, Edward Everett, Irving, and Lowell in America. When in the pages following we anywhere quote usage, it is to the authority of such men that we appeal.

Upon these four sources of help we have drawn in the Revision of "Higher
Lessons" that we now offer to the public.

In this revised work we have given additional reasons for the opinions we hold, and have advanced to some new positions; have explained more fully what some teachers have thought obscure; have qualified what we think was put too positively in former editions; have given the history of constructions where this would deepen interest or aid in composition; have quoted the verdicts of usage on many locutions condemned by purists; have tried to work into the pupil's style the felicities of expression found in the lesson sentences; have taught the pupil earlier in the work, and more thoroughly, the structure and the function of paragraphs; and have led him on from the composition of single sentences of all kinds to the composition of these great groups of sentences. But the distinctive features of "Higher Lessons" that have made the work so useful and so popular stand as they have stood—the Study of Words from their Offices in the Sentence, Analysis for the sake of subsequent Synthesis, Easy Gradation, the Subdivisions and Modifications of the Parts of Speech after the treatment of these in the Sentence, etc., etc. We confess to some surprise that so little of what was thought good in matter and method years ago has been seriously affected by criticism since.

The additions made to "Higher Lessons"—additions that bring the work up to the latest requirements—are generally in foot-notes to pages, and sometimes are incorporated into the body of the Lessons, which in number and numbering remain as they were. The books of former editions and those of this revised edition can, therefore, be used in the same class without any inconvenience.

Of the teachers who have given us invaluable assistance in this Revision, we wish specially to name Prof. Henry M. Worrell, of the Polytechnic Institute; and in this edition of the work, as in the preceding, we take pleasure in acknowledging our great indebtedness to our critic, the distinguished Prof. Francis A. March, of Lafayette College.

* * * * *

LESSON 1.

A TALK ON LANGUAGE.

Let us talk to-day about a language that we never learn from a grammar or from a book of any kind—a language that we come by naturally, and use without thinking of it.

It is a universal language, and consequently needs no interpreter. People of all lands and of all degrees of culture use it; even the brute animals in some measure understand it.

This Natural language is the language of cries, laughter, and tones, the language of the eyes, the nose, the mouth, the whole face; the language of gestures and postures.

The child's cry tells of its wants; its sob, of grief; its scream, of pain; its laugh, of delight. The boy raises his eyebrows in surprise and his nose in disgust, leans forward in expectation, draws back in fear, makes a fist in anger, and calls or drives away his dog simply by the tone in which he speaks.

But feelings and desires are not the only things we wish to communicate. Early in life we begin to acquire knowledge and learn to think, and then we feel the need of a better language.

Suppose, for instance, you have formed an idea of a day; could you express this by a tone, a look, or a gesture?

If you wish to tell me the fact that *yesterday was cloudy,* or that *the days are shorter in winter than in summer,* you find it wholly impossible to do this by means of Natural language.

To communicate, then, your thoughts, or even the mental pictures we have called ideas, you need a language more nearly perfect.

This language is made up of words.

These words you learn from your mothers, and so Word language is your mother-tongue. You learn them, also, from your friends and teachers, your playmates and companions, and you learn them by reading; for words, as you know, may be written as well as spoken.

This Word language we may, from its superiority, call +Language Proper+.

Natural language, as was said, precedes this Word language, but gives way as Word language comes in and takes its place; yet Natural language may be used, and always should be used, to assist and strengthen Word language. In earnest conversation we enforce what we say in words, by the tone in which we utter them, by the varying expression of the face, and by the movements of the different parts of the body.

The look or the gesture may even dart ahead of the word, or it may contradict it, and thus convict the speaker of ignorance or deception.

The happy union of the two kinds of language is the charm of all good reading and speaking. The teacher of elocution is ever trying to recall the pupil to the tones, the facial expression, and the action, so natural to him in childhood and in animated conversation.

+DEFINITION.—*Language Proper* consists of the spoken and the written words used to communicate ideas and thoughts+.

+DEFINITION.—*English Grammar* is the science which teaches the forms, uses, and relations of the words of the English language.+

* * * * *

LESSON 2.

A TALK ON THOUGHTS AND SENTENCES.

To express a thought we use more than a single word, and the words arranged to express a thought we call a sentence.

But there was a time when, through lack of words, we compressed our thought into a single word. The child says to his father, *up*, meaning, *Take me up into your lap*; or, *book*, meaning, *This thing in my hand is a book*.

These first words always deal with the things that can be learned by the senses; they express the child's ideas of these things.

We have spoken of thoughts and sentences; let us see now whether we can find out what a thought is, and what a sentence is.

A sentence is a group of words expressing a thought; it is a body of which a thought is the soul. It is something that can be seen or heard, while a thought cannot be. Let us see whether, in studying a sentence, we may not learn what a thought is.

In any such sentence as this, *Spiders spin*, something is said, or asserted, about something. Here it is said, or asserted, of the animals, spiders, that they spin.

The sentence, then, consists of two parts,—the name of that of which something is said, and that which is said of it.

The first of these parts we call the +Subject+ of the sentence; the second, the +Predicate+.

Now, if the sentence, composed of two parts, expresses the thought, there must be in the thought two parts to be expressed. And there are two: viz., something of which we think, and that which we think of it. In the thought expressed by *Spiders spin*, the animals, spiders, are the something of which we think, and their spinning is what we think of them. In the sentence expressing this thought, the word *spiders* names that of which we think, and the word *spin* tells what we think of spiders.

Not every group of words is necessarily a sentence, because it may not be the expression of a thought. *Spiders spinning* is not a sentence. There is nothing in this expression to show that we have formed a judgment, *i.e.*, that we have really made up our minds that spiders do spin. The spinning is not asserted of the spiders.

Soft feathers, *The shining sun* are not sentences, and for similar reasons. *Feathers are soft*, *The sun shines* are sentences. Here the asserting word is supplied, and something is said of something else.

The shines sun is not a sentence; for, though it contains the asserting word *shines*, the arrangement is such that no assertion is made, and no thought is expressed.

* * * * *

LESSON 3.

A TALK ON SOUNDS AND LETTERS.

We have already told you that in expressing our ideas and thoughts we use two kinds of words, spoken words and written words.

We learned the spoken words first. Mankind spoke long before they wrote. Not until people wished to communicate with those at a distance, or had thought out something worth handing down to aftertimes, did they need to write.

But speaking was easy. The air, the lungs, and the organs of the throat and mouth were at hand. The first cry was a suggestion. Sounds and noises were heard on every side, provoking imitation, and the need of speech for the purposes of communication was imperative.

Spoken words are made up of sounds. There are over forty sounds in the English language. The different combinations of these give us all the words of our spoken tongue. That you may clearly understand these sounds, we will tell you something about the human voice.

In talking, the air driven out from your lungs beats against two flat muscles, stretched, like bands, across the top of the windpipe, and causes them to vibrate up and down. This vibration makes sound. Take a thread, put one end between your teeth, hold the other with thumb and finger, draw it tight and strike it, and you will understand how voice is made. The shorter the string, or the tighter it is drawn, the faster will it vibrate, and the higher will be the pitch of the sound. The more violent the blow, the farther will the string vibrate, and the louder will be the sound. Just so with these vocal bands or cords. The varying force with which the breath strikes them and their different tensions and lengths at different times, explain the different degrees of loudness and the varying pitch of the voice.

If the voice thus produced comes out through the mouth held well open, a class of sounds is formed which we call vowel sounds.

But if the voice is held back or obstructed by the palate, tongue, teeth, or lips, one kind of the sounds called consonant sounds is made. If the breath is driven out without voice, and is held back by these same parts of the mouth, the other kind of consonant sounds is formed.

The written word is made up of characters, or letters, which represent to the eye these sounds that address the ear.

You are now prepared to understand us when we say that +vowels+ are the +letters+ that stand for the +open sounds+ of the +voice+, and that +consonants+ are the +letters+ that stand for the sounds made by the +obstructed voice+ and the +obstructed breath+.

The alphabet of a language is a complete list of its letters. A perfect alphabet would have one letter for each sound, and only one.

Our alphabet is imperfect in at least these three ways:—

1. Some of the letters are superfluous; *c* stands for the sound of *s* or of *k*, as in *city* and *can*; *q* has the sound of *k*, as in *quit*; and *x* that of *ks*, *gz*, or *z*, as in *expel*, *exist*, and *Xenophon*.

2. Combinations of letters sometimes represent single sounds; as, *th* in *thine*, *th* in *thin*, *ng* in *sing*, and *sh* in *shut*.

3. Some letters stand each for many sounds. Twenty-three letters represent over forty sounds. Every vowel does more than single duty; *e* stands for two sounds, as in *mete* and *met*; *i* for two, as in *pine* and *pin*; *o* for three, as in *note*, *not*, and *move*; *u* for four, as in *tube*, *tub*, *full*, and *fur*; *a* for six, as in *fate*, *fat*, *far*, *fall*, *fast*, and *fare*.

W is a vowel when it unites with a preceding vowel to represent a vowel sound, and *y* is a vowel when it has the sound of *i*, as in *now, by, boy, newly*. *W* and *y* are consonants at the beginning of a word or syllable.

The various sounds of the several vowels and even of the same vowel are caused by the different shapes which the mouth assumes. These changes in its cavity produce, also, the two sounds that unite in each of the compounds, *ou, oi, ew,* and in the alphabetic *i* and *o*.

       1. 2.

Vocal Consonants. Aspirates.

    b…………….p
    d…………….t
    g…………….k
    ————————-h
    j…………….ch
    l————————
    m————————
    n————————
    r————————
    th……………..th
 (in *thine*) (in *thin*)
    v……………..f
    w————————
    y————————
    z (in *zone*)……s
    z (in *azure*)…..sh

The consonants in column 1 represent the sounds made by the obstructed voice; those in column 2, except *h* (which represents a mere forcible breathing), represent those made by the obstructed breath.

The letters are mostly in pairs. Now note that the tongue, teeth, lips, and palate are placed in the same relative position to make the sounds of both letters in any pair. The difference in the sounds of the letters of any pair is simply this: there is voice in the sounds of the letters in column 1, and only whisper in those of column 2. Give the sound of any letter in column 1, as *b, g, v*, and the last or vanishing part of it is the sound of the other letter of the pair.

TO THE TEACHER.—Write these letters on the board, as above, and drill the pupils on the sounds till they can see and make these distinctions. Drill them on the vowels also.

In closing this talk with you, we wish to emphasize one point brought before you. Here is a pencil, a real thing; we carry in memory a picture of the pencil, which we call an idea; and there are the two words naming this idea, the spoken and the written. Learn to distinguish clearly these four things.

TO THE TEACHER.—In reviewing these three Lessons, put particular emphasis on Lesson 2.

* * * * *

LESSON 4.

ANALYSIS AND THE DIAGRAM.

TO THE TEACHER.—If the pupils have been through "Graded Lessons" or its equivalent, some of the following Lessons may be passed over rapidly.

+DEFINITION.—A *Sentence* is the expression of a thought in words+.

+Direction+.—*Analyze the following sentences*:—

+Model+.—*Spiders spin.* Why is this a sentence? Ans.—Because it expresses a thought. Of what is something thought? Ans.—Spiders. Which word tells what is thought? Ans.—*Spin.* [Footnote: The word *spiders*, standing in Roman, names our idea of the real thing; *spin*, used merely as a word, is in Italics. This use of Italics the teacher and the pupil will please note here and elsewhere.]

1. Tides ebb. 2. Liquids flow. 3. Steam expands. 4. Carbon burns. 5. Iron melts. 6. Powder explodes. 7. Leaves tremble. 8. Worms crawl. 9. Hares leap.

In each of these sentences there are, as you have learned, two parts—the +Subject+ and the +Predicate+.

+DEFINITION+.—The *Subject of a sentence* names that of which something is thought.+

+DEFINITION+.—The *Predicate of a sentence* tells what is thought.+

+DEFINITION+.—The *Analysis of a sentence* is the separation of it into its parts.+

+Direction+.—*Analyze these sentences:*—

+Model+.—*Beavers build.* This is a sentence because it expresses a thought. *Beavers* is the subject because it names that of which something is thought; *build* is the predicate because it tells what is thought. [Footnote: When pupils are familiar with the definitions, let the form of analysis be varied. The reasons may be made more specific. Here and elsewhere avoid mechanical repetition.]

1. Squirrels climb. 2. Blood circulates. 3. Muscles tire. 4. Heralds proclaim. 5. Apes chatter. 6. Branches wave. 7. Corn ripens. 8. Birds twitter.

9. Hearts throb.

+Explanation+.—Draw a heavy line and divide it into two parts. Let the first part represent the subject of a sentence; the second, the predicate.

If you write a word over the first part, you will understand that this word is the subject of a sentence. If you write a word over the second part, you will understand that this word is the predicate of a sentence.

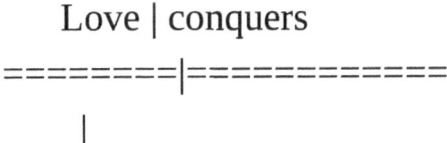

You see, by looking at this figure, that *Love conquers* is a sentence; that *love* is the subject, and *conquers* the predicate.

Such figures, made up of straight lines, we call *Diagrams*.

+DEFINITION.—A *Diagram* is a picture of the offices and the relations of the different parts of a sentence.+

+Direction+.—*Analyze these sentences*:—

1. Frogs croak. 2. Hens sit. 3. Sheep bleat. 4. Cows low. 5. Flies buzz. 6. Sap ascends. 7. Study pays. 8. Buds swell. 9. Books aid. 10. Noise disturbs. 11. Hope strengthens. 12. Cocks crow.

* * * * *

LESSON 5.

COMPOSITION—SUBJECT AND PREDICATE.

+CAPITAL LETTER—RULE.—The first word of every sentence must begin with a *capital letter*+.

+PERIOD—RULE.—A *period* must be placed after every sentence that simply affirms, denies, or commands.+

+Direction+.—*Construct sentences by supplying a subject to each of the following predicates*:—

Ask yourselves the questions, What tarnishes? Who sailed, conquered, etc.?

1. —— tarnishes. 2. —— capsize. 3. —— radiates. 4. —— sentence. 5. —— careen. 6. —— sailed. 7. —— descends. 8. —— glisten. 9. —— absorb. 10. —— corrode. 11. —— conquered. 12. —— surrendered. 13. —— refines. 14. —— gurgle. 15. —— murmur.

+Direction+.—*Construct sentences by supplying a predicate to each of the following subjects*:—

Ask yourselves the question, Glycerine does what?

1. Glycerine ——. 2. Yankees ——. 3. Tyrants ——. 4. Pendulums ——. 5. Caesar ——. 6. Labor ——. 7. Chalk ——. 8. Nature ——. 9. Tempests ——. 10. Seeds ——. 11. Heat ——. 12. Philosophers ——. 13. Bubbles ——. 14. Darkness ——. 15. Wax ——. 16. Reptiles ——. 17. Merchants ——. 18. Meteors ——. 19. Conscience ——. 20. Congress ——. 21. Life ——. 22. Vapors ——. 23. Music ——. 24. Pitch ——.

TO THE TEACHER.—This exercise may profitably be extended by supplying several subjects to each predicate, and several predicates to each subject.

* * * * *

LESSON 6.

ANALYSIS.

The predicate sometimes contains more than one word.

+Direction+.—*Analyze as in Lesson 4.*

1. Moisture is exhaled. 2. Conclusions are drawn. 3. Industry will enrich. 4. Stars have disappeared. 5. Twilight is falling. 6. Leaves are turning. 7. Sirius has appeared. 8. Constantinople had been captured. 9. Electricity has been harnessed. 10. Tempests have been raging. 11. Nuisances should be abated. 12. Jerusalem was destroyed. 13. Light can be reflected. 14. Rain must have fallen. 15. Planets have been discovered. 16. Palaces shall crumble. 17. Storms may be gathering. 18. Essex might have been saved. 19. Caesar could have been crowned, 20. Inventors may be encouraged.

+Direction+.—*Point out the subject and the predicate of each sentence in Lessons 12 and 17.*

Look first for the word that asserts, and then, by putting *who* or *what* before this predicate, the subject may easily be found.

TO THE TEACHER.—Let this exercise be continued till the pupils can readily point out the subject and the predicate in ordinary simple sentences.

When this can be done promptly, the first and most important step in analysis will have been taken.

* * * * *

LESSON 7.

COMPOSITION—SUBJECT AND PREDICATE.

+Direction+.—*Make at least ten good sentences out of the words in the three columns following:*—

The helping words in column 2 must be prefixed to words in column 3 in order to make complete predicates. Analyze your sentences.

1 2 3
Arts is progressing.
Allen was tested.
Life are command.
Theories will prolonged.
Science would released.
Truth were falling.
Shadows may be burned.
Moscow has been measured.
Raleigh have been prevail.
Quantity should have been lost.

Review Questions.

What is language proper? What is English grammar? What is a sentence? What are its two parts? What is the subject of a sentence? The predicate of a sentence? The analysis of a sentence? What is a diagram? What rule has been given for the use of capital letters? For the period? May the predicate contain more than one word? Illustrate.

TO THE TEACHER.—Introduce the class to the Parts of Speech before the close of this recitation. See "Introductory Hints" below.

* * * * *

LESSON 8.

CLASSES OF WORDS.

NOUNS.

+Introductory Hints+.—We have now reached the point where we must classify the words of our language. But we are appalled by their number. If we must learn all about the forms and the uses of a hundred thousand words by studying these words one by one, we shall die ignorant of English grammar.

But may we not deal with words as we do with plants? If we had to study and name each leaf and stem and flower, taken singly, we should never master the botany even of our garden-plants.

But God has made things to resemble one another and to differ from one another; and, as he has given us the power to detect resemblances and differences, we are able to group things that have like qualities.

From certain likenesses in form and in structure, we put certain flowers together and call them roses; from other likenesses, we get another class called lilies; from others still, violets. Just so we classify trees and get the oak, the elm, the maple, etc.

The myriad objects of nature fall into comparatively few classes. Studying each class, we learn all we need to know of every object in it.

From their likenesses, though not in form, we classify words. We group them according to their similarities in use, or office, in the sentence. Sorting them thus, we find that they all fall into eight classes, which we call Parts of Speech.

We find that many words name things—are the names of things of which we can think and speak. These we place in one class and call them +Nouns+ (Latin *nomen*, a name, a noun).

PRONOUNS.

Without the little words which we shall italicize, it would be difficult for one stranger to ask another, "Can *you* tell *me who* is the postmaster at B?" The one would not know what name to use instead of *you*, the other would not recognize the name in the place of *me*, and both would be puzzled to find a substitute for *who*.

I, you, my, me, what, we, it, he, who, him, she, them, and other words are used in place of nouns, and are, therefore, called +Pronouns+ (Lat. *pro*, for, and *nomen*, a noun).

By means of these handy little words we can represent any or every object in existence. We could hardly speak or write without them now, they so frequently shorten the expression and prevent confusion and repetition.

+DEFINITION.—A *Noun* is the name of anything.+

+DEFINITION.—A *Pronoun* is a word used for a noun.+

The principal office of nouns is to name the things of which we say, or assert, something in the sentence.

+Direction+.—*Write, according to the model, the names of things that can burn, grow, melt, love, roar, or revolve.*

+Model.+— *Nouns.*
  Wood |
  Paper |

    Oil |
    Houses + burn or burns.
    Coal |
    Leaves |
    Matches |
    Clothes |

+Remark.+—Notice that, when the subject adds *s* or *es* to denote more than one, the predicate does not take *s*. Note how it would sound if both should add *s*.

+Every subject+ of a sentence is a +noun+, or some word or words used as a noun. But not every noun in a sentence is a subject.

+Direction.+—*Select and write all the nouns and pronouns, whether subjects or not, in the sentences given in Lesson* 18.

In writing them observe the following rules:—

+CAPITAL LETTER—RULE.—*Proper,* or *individual, names* and *words derived from them* begin with capital letters.+

+PERIOD and CAPITAL LETTER—RULE.—*Abbreviations* generally begin with capital letters and are always followed by the period.+

* * * * *

LESSON 9.

CAPITAL LETTERS.

+Direction.+—*From the following words select and write in one column those names that distinguish individual things from others of the same class, and in another column those words that are derived from individual names:—*

Observe Rule 1, Lesson 8.

ohio, state, chicago, france, bostonian, country, england, boston, milton, river, girl, mary, hudson, william, britain, miltonic, city, englishman, messiah, platonic, american, deity, bible, book, plato, christian, broadway, america, jehovah, british, easter, europe, man, scriptures, god.

+Direction.+—*Write the names of the days of the week and the months of the year, beginning each with a capital letter; and write the names of the seasons without capital letters.*

+Remember+ that, when a class name and a distinguishing word combine to make one individual name, each word begins with a capital letter; as, *Jersey City*. [Footnote: *Dead Sea* is composed of the class name *sea*, which applies to all seas, and the word *Dead*, which distinguishes one sea from all others.]

But, when the distinguishing word can by itself be regarded as a complete name, the class name begins with a small letter; as, *river Rhine*.

+Examples+.—Long Island, Good Friday, Mount Vernon, Suspension Bridge, New
York city, Harper's Ferry, Cape May, Bunker Hill, Red River, Lake Erie, General Jackson, White Mountains, river Thames, Astor House, steamer Drew,
North Pole.

+Direction+.—*Write these words, using capital letters when needed:—*

ohio river, professor huxley, president adams, doctor brown, clinton county, westchester county, colonel burr, secretary stanton, lake george, green mountains, white sea, cape cod, delaware bay, atlantic ocean, united states, rhode island.

+Remember+ that, when an individual name is made up of a class name, the word *of,* and a distinguishing word, the class name and the distinguishing word should each begin with a capital letter; as, *Gulf of Mexico.* But, when the distinguishing word can by itself be regarded as a complete name, the class name should begin with a small letter; as, *city of London.* [Footnote: The need of some definite instruction to save the young writer from hesitation and confusion in the use of capitals is evident from the following variety of forms now in use: *City* of New York, *city* of New York, New York *City,* New York *city,* New York *State,* New York *state,* Fourth *Avenue,* Fourth *avenue,* Grand *Street,* Grand *street,* Grand *st.,* Atlantic *Ocean,* Atlantic *ocean,* Mediterranean *Sea,* Mediterranean *sea,* Kings *County,* Kings *county,* etc.

The usage of newspapers and of text-books on geography would probably favor the writing of the class names in the examples above with initial capitals; but we find in the most carefully printed books and periodicals a tendency to favor small letters in such cases.

In the superscription of letters, such words as *street, city,* and *county* begin with capitals.

Usage certainly favors small initials for the following italicized words: *river* Rhine, Catskill *village,* the Ohio and Mississippi *rivers.* If *river* and *village,* in the preceding examples, are not essential parts of the individual names, why should *river, ocean,* and *county,* in Hudson *river,* Pacific *ocean,* Queens *county,* be treated differently? We often say the *Hudson,* the *Pacific, Queens,* without adding the explanatory class name.

The principle we suggest may be in advance of common usage; but it is in the line of progress, and it tends to uniformity of practice and to an improved appearance of the page. About a century ago every noun began with a capital letter.

The American Cyclopedia takes a position still further in advance, as illustrated in the following: Bed *river,* Black *sea, gulf* of Mexico, Rocky *mountains.* In the Encyclopaedia Britannica (Little, Brown, & Co., 9th ed.) we find Connecticut *river,* Madison *county,* etc., quite uniformly; but we find *Gulf* of Mexico, Pacific *Ocean,* etc.]

+Direction+.—*Write these words, using capital letters when needed:*—

city of atlanta, isle of man, straits of dover, state of Vermont, isthmus of darien, sea of galilee, queen of england, bay of naples, empire of china.

+Remember+ that, when a compound name is made up of two or more distinguishing words, as, Henry Clay, John Stuart Mill, each word begins with a capital letter.

+Direction+.—*Write these words, using capital letters when needed:*—

great britain, lower california, south carolina, daniel webster, new england, oliver wendell holmes, north america, new orleans, james russell lowell, british america.

+Remember+ that, in writing the titles of books, essays, poems, plays, etc., and the names of the Deity, only the chief words begin with capital letters; as, Decline and Fall of the Roman Empire, Supreme Being, Paradise Lost, the Holy One of Israel.

+Direction+.—*Write these words, using capital letters when needed:*—

declaration of independence, clarendon's history of the great rebellion, webster's reply to hayne, pilgrim's progress, johnson's lives of the poets, son of man, the most high, dombey and son, tent on the beach, bancroft's history of the united states.

+Direction+.—*Write these miscellaneous names, using capital letters when needed*:—

erie canal, governor tilden, napoleon bonaparte, cape of good hope, pope's essay on criticism, massachusetts bay, city of boston, continent of america, new testament, goldsmith's she stoops to conquer, milton's hymn on the nativity, indian ocean, cape cod bay, plymouth rock, anderson's history of the united states, mount washington, english channel, the holy spirit, new york central railroad, old world, long island sound, flatbush village.

* * * * *

LESSON 10.

ABBREVIATIONS.

+Direction+.—*Some words occur frequently, and for convenience may he abbreviated in writing. Observing Rule 2, Lesson 8, abbreviate these words by writing the first five letters*:—

Thursday and lieutenant.

These by writing the first four letters:—

Connecticut, captain, Colorado, Kansas, Massachusetts, Michigan, Minnesota,

Mississippi, Nebraska, Oregon, professor, president, Tennessee, and Tuesday.

These by writing the first three letters:—

Alabama, answer, Arkansas, California, colonel, Delaware, England, esquire,
Friday, general, George, governor, honorable, Illinois, Indiana, major, Monday, Nevada, reverend, Saturday, secretary, Sunday, Texas, Wednesday, Wisconsin, and the names of the months except May, June, and July.

These by writing the first two letters:—

Company, county, credit, example, and idem (the same).

These by writing the first letter:—

East, north, south, and west. [Footnote: When these words refer to sections of the country, they should begin with capitals.]

These by writing the first and the last letter:—

Doctor, debtor, Georgia, junior, Kentucky, Louisiana, Maine, Maryland, Master, Mister, numero (number), Pennsylvania, saint, street, Vermont, and Virginia.

These by writing the first letter of each word of the compound with a period after each letter:—

Artium baccalaureus (bachelor of arts), anno Domini (in the year of our Lord), artium magister (master of arts), ante meridiem (before noon), before Christ, collect on delivery, District (of) Columbia, divinitatis doctor (doctor of divinity), member (of) Congress, medicinae doctor (doctor of medicine), member (of) Parliament, North America, North Carolina, New Hampshire, New Jersey, New York, postmaster, post meridiem (afternoon), post-office, Rhode Island, South Carolina, and United States.

+Direction.+—*The following abbreviations and those you have made should be committed to memory*:—

Acct. *or* acct., account. Bbl. *or* bbl., barrel. Chas., Charles. Fla., Florida. LL. D., legum doctor (doctor of laws).[Footnote: The doubling of the *l* to *ll* and in *LL. D.*, and of *p* in *pp.*, with no period between the letters, comes from pluralizing the nouns *line, lean*, and *page*.] Messrs., messieurs (gentlemen). Mme., madame. Mo., Missouri. Mrs., (pronounced missis) mistress. Mts., mountains. Ph.D., philosophiae doctor (doctor of philosophy). Recd., received. Robt., Robert. Supt., superintendent. Thos., Thomas. bu., bushel. do., ditto (the same) doz., dozen. e.g., exempli gratia (for example) etc., et caetera (and others). ft., foot, feet. hhd., hogshead. hdkf., handkerchief. i.e., id est (that is). l., line. ll., lines. lb., libra (pound). oz., ounce. p., page. pp., pages. qt., quart. vs., versus (against). viz., videlicet (namely). yd., yard.

+Remark.+—In this Lesson we have given the abbreviations of the states as now regulated by the "U. S. Official Postal Guide." In the "Guide" *Iowa* and *Ohio* are not abbreviated. They are, however, frequently abbreviated thus: *Iowa, Ia.* or *Io.; Ohio, 0.*

The similarity, when hurriedly written, of the abbreviations *Cal., Col.; Ia., Io.; Neb., Nev.; Penn., Tenn.*, etc., has led to much confusion.

* * * * *

LESSON 11.

VERBS.

+Introductory Hints+.—We told you in Lesson 8 how, by noticing the essential likenesses in things and grouping the things thus alike, we could throw the countless objects around us into comparatively few classes.

We began to classify words according to their use, or office, in the sentence; we found one class of words that name things, and we called them *nouns*.

But in all the sentences given you, we have had to use another class of words. These words, you notice, tell what the things do, or assert that they are, or exist.

When we say *Clocks tick*, *tick* is not the name of anything; it tells what clocks do: it asserts action.

When we say *Clocks are*, or *There are clocks*, *are* is not the name of. anything, nor does it tell what clocks do; it simply asserts existence, or being.

When we say *Clocks hang, stand, last, lie*, or *remain*, these words *hang, stand, last*, etc., do not name anything, nor do they tell that clocks act or simply exist; they tell the condition, or state, in which clocks are, or exist; that is, they assert state of being.

All words that assert action, being, or state of being, we call +Verbs+ (+Lat+. *verbum*, a word). The name was given to this class because it was thought that they were the most important words in the sentence.

Give several verbs that assert action. Give some that assert being, and some that assert state of being.

+DEFINITION+.—+A *Verb* is a word that asserts action, being-, or state of being+.

There are, however, two forms of the verb, the participle and the infinitive (see Lessons 37 and 40), that express action, being, or state of being, without asserting it.

+Direction.+—*Write after each of the following nouns as many appropriate verbs as you can think of:*—

Let some express being and some express state of being.

+Model.—*Noun.*
```
        | burns.
        | melt.
        | scorches.
   Fire | keep.
   (or) + spreads.
   Fires | glow.
        | rages.
        | heat.
        | exists.
```

+Remark.+—Notice that the simple form of the verb, as, *burn, melt, scorch,* adds *s* or *es* when its subject noun names but one thing.

Lawyers, mills, horses, books, education, birds, mind.

A verb may consist of two, three, or even four words; as, *is learning, may be learned, could have been learned.* [Footnote: Such groups of words are sometimes called *verb-phrases.* For definition of *phrase,* see Lesson 17.]

+Direction.+—*Unite the words in columns 2 and 3 below, and append the verbs thus formed to the nouns and pronouns in column 1 so as to make good sentences:*—

+Remark.+—Notice that *is, was,* and *has* are used with nouns naming one thing, and with the pronouns *he, she,* and *it*; and that *are, were,* and *have* are used with nouns naming more than one thing, and with the pronouns *we, you,* and *they. I* may be used with *am, was,* and *have.*

1 2 3
Words am confused.
Cotton is exported.
Sugar are refined.
Air coined.
Teas was delivered.
Speeches were weighed.
I, we, you has been imported.
He, she, it, they have been transferred.

As verbs are the only words that assert, +every predicate+ must be a verb, or must contain a verb.

+Naming the class+ to which a word belongs is the +first step in parsing.+

+Direction+.—*Parse five of the sentences you have written.*

+Model+.—*Poland was dismembered.*

+Parsing+.—*Poland* is a noun because ——; *was dismembered* is a verb because it asserts action.

* * * * *

LESSON 12.

MODIFIED SUBJECT.

ADJECTIVES.

+Introductory Hints+.—The subject noun and the predicate verb are not always or often the whole of the structure that we call the sentence, though they are the underlying timbers that support the rest of the verbal bridge. Other words may be built upon them.

We learned in Lesson 8 that things resemble one another and differ from one another. They resemble and they differ in what we call their qualities. Things are alike whose qualities are the same, as, two oranges having the same color, taste, and odor. Things are unlike, as an orange and an apple, whose qualities are different.

It is by their qualities, then, that we know things and group them.

Ripe apples are healthful. Unripe apples are hurtful. In these two sentences we have the same word apples to name the same general class of things; but the prefixed words ripe and unripe, marking opposite qualities in the apples, separate the apples into two kinds—the ripe ones and the unripe ones.

These prefixed words *ripe* and *unripe*, then, limit the word *apples* in its scope; *ripe apples* or *unripe apples* applies to fewer things than *apples* alone applies to.

If we say *the, this, that* apple, or *an, no* apple, or *some, many, eight* apples, we do not mark any quality of the fruit; but *the, this,* or *that* points out a particular apple, and limits the word *apple* to the one pointed out; and *an, no, some, many,* or *eight* limits the word in respect to the number of apples that it denotes.

These and all such words as by marking quality, by pointing out, or by specifying number or quantity limit the scope or add to the meaning of the noun, +modify+ it, and are called +Modifiers+.

In the sentence above, *apples* is the +Simple Subject+ and *ripe apples* is the +Modified Subject+.

Words that modify nouns and pronouns are called +Adjectives+ (Lat. *ad*, to, and *jacere*, to throw).

+DEFINITION.+—A *Modifier* is a word or a group of words joined to some part of the sentence to qualify or limit the meaning+.

The +Subject+ with its +Modifiers+ is called the +Modified Subject+, or *Logical Subject*.

+DEFINITION.+—An *Adjective* is a word used to modify a noun or a pronoun+.

Analysis and Parsing.

1. The cold November rain is falling.

```
            rain | is falling
=============================|===============
\The \cold \November |
```

+Explanation.+—The two lines shaded alike and placed uppermost stand for the subject and the predicate, and show that these are of the same rank, and are the principal parts of the sentence. The lighter lines, placed under and joined to the subject line, stand for the less important parts, the modifiers, and show what is modified. [Footnote: TO THE TEACHER.—When several adjectives are joined to one noun, each adjective does not always modify the unlimited noun. *That old wooden house was burned.*

Here *wooden* modifies *house,* *old* modifies *house* limited by *wooden,* and *that* modifies *house* limited by *old* and *wooden.* This may be illustrated in the diagram by numbering the modifiers in the order of their rank, thus:—

```
                  |
===================|=======
 \3 \2 \1 |
```

Adverbs, and both phrase and clause modifiers often differ in rank in the same way. If the pupils are able to see these distinctions, it will be well to have them made in the analysis, as they often determine the punctuation and the arrangement. See Lessons 13 and 21.]

+TO THE TEACHER.+—While we, from experience, are clear in the belief that diagrams are very helpful in the analysis of sentences, we wish to say that the work required in this book can all be done without resorting to these figures. If some other form, or no form, of written analysis is preferred, our diagrams can be omitted without break or confusion.

When diagrams are used, only the teacher can determine how many shall be required in any one Lesson, and how soon the pupil may dispense with their aid altogether.

+Oral Analysis.+—(Here and hereafter we shall omit from the oral analysis and parsing whatever has been provided for in previous Lessons.) *The, cold,* and *November* are modifiers of the subject. *The cold November rain* is the modified subject.

TO THE TEACHER.—While in these "models" we wish to avoid repetition, we should require of the pupils full forms of oral analysis for at

+Oral Analysis+.—*Very quietly* is a modifier of the predicate; *quietly* is the principal word of the group; *very* modifies *quietly*; *the leaves* is the modified subject; *fall very quietly* is the modified predicate.

+Parsing+.—*Quietly* is an adverb modifying *fall*, telling the manner; *very* is an adverb modifying *quietly*, telling the degree.

2. The old, historic Charter Oak was blown down. 3. The stern, rigid Puritans often worshiped there. 4. Bright-eyed daisies peep up everywhere. 5. The precious morning hours should not be wasted. 6. The timely suggestion was very kindly received. 7. We turned rather abruptly. 8. A highly enjoyable entertainment was provided. 9. The entertainment was highly enjoyed. 10. Why will people exaggerate so! 11. A somewhat dangerous pass had been reached quite unexpectedly. 12. We now travel still more rapidly. 13. Therefore he spoke excitedly. 14. You will undoubtedly be very cordially welcomed. 15. A furious equinoctial gale has just swept by. 16. The Hell Gate reef was slowly drilled away.

* * * * *

LESSON 15.

COMPOSITION—ADVERBS.

+Caution+.—So place adverbs that there can be no doubt as to what you intend them to modify. Have regard to the sound also.

+Direction+.—*Place the, italicized words below in different positions, and note the effect on the sound and the sense:—*

1. I *immediately* ran out. 2. *Only* one was left there. 3. She looked down *proudly*. 4. *Unfortunately*, this assistance came too late.

+Direction+.—*Construct on each of these subjects three sentences having modified subjects and modified predicates:—*

For punctuation, see Lesson 21.

+Model+. —— *clouds* ——. 1. *Dark, heavy, threatening clouds are slowly gathering above.* 2. *Those, brilliant, crimson clouds will very soon dissolve.* 3. *Thin, fleecy clouds are scudding over.*

1. —— ocean ——. 2. —— breeze ——. 3. —— shadows ——. 4. —— rock ——. 5. —— leaves ——.

+Direction+.—*Compose sentences in which these adverbs shall modify verbs:—*

Heretofore, hereafter, annually, tenderly, inaudibly, legibly, evasively, everywhere, aloof, forth.

+Direction+.—*Compose sentences in which five of these adverbs shall modify adjectives, and five shall modify adverbs:—*

Far, unusually, quite, altogether, slightly, somewhat, much, almost, too, rather.

* * * * *

LESSON 16.

REVIEW.

TO THE TEACHER.—In all school work, but especially here, where the philosophy of the sentence and the principles of construction are developed in progressive steps, success depends largely on the character of the reviews.

Let reviews be, so far as possible, topical. Require frequent outlines of the work passed over, especially of what is taught in the "Introductory Hints." The language, except that of Rules and Definitions, should be the pupil's own, and the illustrative sentences should be original.

+Direction+.—*Review from Lesson 8 to Lesson 15, inclusive.*

Give the substance of the "Introductory Hints" (tell, for example, what three things such words as *tick, are,* and *remain* do in the sentence, what office they have in common, what such words are called, and why; what common office such words as *ripe, the,* and *eight* have, in what three ways they perform it, what such words are called, and why, etc.). Repeat and illustrate definitions and rules; illustrate what is taught of the capitalization and the abbreviation of names, and of the position of adjectives and adverbs.

Exercises on the Composition of the Sentence and the Paragraph.

(SEE PAGES 150-153.)

TO THE TEACHER.—After the pupil has learned a few principles of analysis and construction through the aid of short detached sentences that exclude everything unfamiliar, he may be led to recognize these same principles in longer related sentences grouped into paragraphs. The study of paragraphs selected for this purpose may well be extended as an informal preparation for what is afterwards formally presented in the regular lessons of the text-book.

These "Exercises" are offered only as suggestions. The teacher must, of course, determine where and how often this composition should be introduced.

We invite special attention to the study of the paragraph.

* * * *

LESSON 17.

PREPOSITIONAL PHRASES AND PREPOSITIONS.

+Introductory Hints+.—To express our thoughts with greater exactness we may need to expand a word modifier into several words; as, A *long* ride brought us *there* = A ride *of one hundred miles* brought us *to Chicago*. These groups of words, *of one hundred miles* and *to Chicago*—the one substituted for the adjective *long*, the other for the adverb *there*—we call +Phrases+. A phrase that does the work of an adjective is called an +Adjective Phrase+. A phrase that does the work of an adverb is called an +Adverb Phrase+.

As adverbs modify adjectives and adverbs, they may modify their equivalent phrases; as, The train stops *only at the station*. They sometimes modify only the introductory word of the phrase—this introductory word being adverbial in its nature; as, He sailed *nearly around* the globe.

That we may learn the office of such words as *of, to,* and *at,* used to introduce these phrases, let us see how the relation of one idea to another may be expressed. *Wealthy men*. These two words express two ideas as related. We have learned to know this relation by the form and position of the words. Change these, and the relation is lost—*men wealth*. But by using *of* before *wealth* the relation is restored—-*men of wealth*. The word *of*, then, shows the relation between the ideas expressed by the words *men* and *wealth*.

All such relation words are called +Prepositions+ (Lat. *prae*, before, and *positus*, placed—their usual position being before the noun with which they form a phrase).

A phrase introduced by a preposition is called a +Prepositional Phrase+. This, however, is not the only kind of phrase.

+DEFINITION.+—A *Phrase* is a group of words denoting related ideas, and having a distinct office, but not expressing a thought+.

+DEFINITION.+—A *Preposition* is a word that introduces a phrase modifier, and shows the relation, in sense, of its principal word to the word modified.+

Analysis and Parsing.

1. The pitch of the musical note depends upon the rapidity of vibration.

TO THE TEACHER.—See suggestions in Lesson 12, concerning the use of diagrams.

```
    pitch depends
==========|==================
\The \of \upon
    \ \
     \ note \ rapidity
      \———— \—————
       \the \musical \the \of
                      \
                      \vibration
                       \————-
```

+Explanation+.—The diagram of the phrase is made up of a slanting line standing for the introductory word, and a horizontal line representing the principal word. Under the latter are drawn the lines which represent the modifiers of the principal word.

+Oral Analysis+.—-*The* and the adjective phrase *of the musical note* are modifiers of the subject; the adverb phrase *upon the rapidity of vibration* is a modifier of the predicate. *Of* introduces the first phrase, and *note* is the principal word; *the* and *musical* are modifiers of *note*; *upon* introduces the second phrase, and *rapidity* is the principal word; *the* and the adjective phrase *of vibration* are modifiers of *rapidity*; *of* introduces this phrase, and *vibration* is the principal word.

TO THE TEACHER.—See suggestions in Lesson 12, concerning oral analysis.

+Parsing+.—*Of* is a preposition showing the relation, in sense, of *note* to *pitch*; etc., etc.

TO THE TEACHER.—Insist that, in parsing, the pupils shall give specific reasons instead of general definitions.

2. The Gulf Stream can be traced along the shores of the United States by the blueness of the water. 3. The North Pole has been approached in three principal directions. 4. In 1607, Hudson penetrated within six hundred miles of the North Pole. [Footnote: "1607" may be treated as a noun, and "six hundred" as one adjective.] 5. The breezy morning died into silent noon. 6. The Delta of the Mississippi was once at St. Louis. 7. Coal of all kinds has originated from the decay of plants. 8. Genius can breathe freely only in the atmosphere of freedom.

```
   \in \
\_____\below
 \atmosphere \just \
```

```
    _____ \Falls
     \ _____
      \only \
               \the
```

+Explanation+.——*Only* modifies the whole phrase, and *just* modifies the preposition.

9. The Suspension Bridge is stretched across the Niagara river just below the Falls. 10. In Mother Goose the cow jumps clear over the moon. 11. The first standing army was formed in the middle of the fifteenth century. 12. The first astronomical observatory in Europe was erected at Seville by the Saracens. 13. The tails of some comets stretch to the distance of 100,000,000 miles. 14. The body of the great Napoleon was carried back from St. Helena to France.

* * * * *

LESSON 18.

COMPOSITION-PREPOSITIONAL PHRASES.

+COMMA-RULE.—Phrases that are placed out of their usual order [Footnote: For the usual order of words and phrases, see Lesson 51.] and made emphatic, or that are loosely connected with the rest of the sentence, should be set off by the comma.+ [Footnote: An expression in the body of a sentence is set off by two commas; at the beginning or at the end, by one comma.]

+Remark.+—This rule must be applied with caution. Unless it is desired to make the phrase emphatic, or to break the continuity of the thought, the growing usage among writers is not to set it off.

+Direction.+—*Tell why the comma is, or is not, used in these sentences*:—

1. Between the two mountains lies a fertile valley. 2. Of the scenery along the Rhine, many travelers speak with enthusiasm. 3. He went, at the urgent request of the stranger, for the doctor. 4. He went from New York to Philadelphia on Monday. 5. In the dead of night, with a chosen band, under the cover of a truce, he approached.

+Direction+.—*Punctuate such of these sentences as need punctuation*:—

1. England in the eleventh century was conquered by the Normans. 2. Amid the angry yells of the spectators he died. 3. For the sake of emphasis a word or a phrase may be placed out of its natural order. 4. In the Pickwick Papers the conversation of Sam Weller is spiced with wit. 5. New York on the contrary abounds in men of wealth. 6. It has come down by uninterrupted tradition from the earliest times to the present day.

+Direction+.—*See in how many places the phrases in the sentences above may stand without obscuring the thought.*

+Caution+.—So place phrase modifiers that there can be no doubt as to what yon intend them to modify. Have regard to the sound also.

+Direction+.—*Correct these errors in position, and use the comma when needed*:—

1. The honorable member was reproved for being intoxicated by the president. 2. That small man is speaking with red whiskers. 3. A message was read from the President in the Senate. 4. With his gun toward the woods he started in the morning. 5. On Monday evening on temperance by Mr. Gough a lecture at the old brick church was delivered.

+Direction+.—*Form a sentence out of each of these groups of words:*—

(Look sharply to the arrangement and the punctuation.)

1. Of mind of splendor under the garb often is concealed poverty. 2. Of affectation of the young fop in the face impertinent an was seen smile. 3. Has been scattered Bible English the of millions by hundreds of the earth over the face. 4. To the end with no small difficulty of the journey at last through deep roads we after much fatigue came. 5. At the distance a flood of flame from the line from thirty iron mouths of twelve hundred yards of the enemy poured forth.

+Direction+.—*See into how many good, clear sentences you can convert these by transposing the phrases:*—

1. He went over the mountains on a certain day in early boyhood. 2. Ticonderoga was taken from the British by Ethan Allen on the tenth of May in 1775.

* * * * *

LESSON 19.

COMPOSITION—PREPOSITIONAL PHRASES.

+Direction+.—*Rewrite these sentences, changing the italicized words into equivalent phrases:*—

+Model+.—The sentence was *carefully* written. The sentence was written *with* care.

1. A *brazen* image was *then* set up. 2. Those *homeless* children were *kindly* treated. 3. Much has been said about the *Swiss* scenery. 4. An *aerial*

trip to Europe was *rashly* planned. 5. The *American* Continent was *probably* discovered by Cabot.

+Direction+.—*Change these adjectives and adverbs into equivalent phrases; and then, attending carefully to the punctuation, use these phrases in sentences of your own:—*

1. Bostonian 2. why 3. incautiously 4. nowhere 5. there 6. hence 7. northerly 8. national 9. whence 10. here 11. Arabian 12. lengthy 13. historical 14. lucidly 15. earthward

+Direction+.—*Compose sentences, using these phrases as modifiers:—*

Of copper; in Pennsylvania; from the West Indies; around the world; between the tropics; toward the Pacific; on the 22d of February; during the reign of Elizabeth; before the application of steam to machinery; at the Centennial Exposition of 1876.

* * * * *

LESSON 20.

COMPOUND SUBJECT AND COMPOUND PREDICATE.

CONJUNCTIONS AND INTERJECTIONS.

+Introductory Hints.+—*Edward, Mary, and Elizabeth reigned in England.* The three words *Edward, Mary,* and *Elizabeth* have the same predicate—the same act being asserted of the king and the two queens. *Edward, Mary,* and *Elizabeth* are connected by *and, and* being understood between Edward and Mary. Connected subjects having the same predicate form a +Compound Subject+.

Charles I. was seized, was tried, and was beheaded. The three predicates *was seized, was tried,* and *was beheaded* have the same subject—the three acts being asserted of the same king. Connected predicates having the same subject form a +Compound Predicate.+

A sentence may have both a compound subject and a compound predicate; as, *Mary* and *Elizabeth lived* and *reigned* in England.

The words connecting the parts of a compound subject or of a compound predicate are called +Conjunctions+ (Lat. *con*, or *cum*, together, and *jungere*, to join).

A conjunction may connect other parts of the sentence, as two word modifiers—A dark *and* rainy night follows; Some men sin deliberately *and* presumptuously.

It may connect two phrases; as, The equinox occurs in March *and* in September.

It may connect two clauses, that is, expressions that, standing alone, would be sentences; as, The leaves of the pine fall in spring, *but* the leaves of the maple drop in autumn.

+Interjections+ (Lat. *inter*, between, and *jacere*, to throw) are the eighth and last part of speech.

Oh! ah! pooh! pshaw! etc., express bursts of feeling too sudden and violent for deliberate sentences.

_Hail! fudge! indeed! amen! _etc., express condensed thought as well as feeling.

Any part of speech may be wrenched from its construction with other words, and may lapse into an interjection; *as, behold! shame! what!*

Professor Sweet calls interjections *sentence-words*.

Two or more connected subjects having the same predicate form a +Compound Subject+.

Two or more connected predicates having the same subject form a +Compound Predicate+.

+DEFINITION.—A *Conjunction* is a word used to connect words, phrases, or clauses.+

+DEFINITION.—An *Interjection* is a word used to express strong or sudden feeling.+

Analysis and Parsing.

1. Ah! anxious wives, sisters, and mothers wait for the news.

```
          Ah
         ____

wives
========\
    '\
     ' \ | wait
sisters 'x \=====|===========
========' \ \anxious \for
    'and/ \
```

```
         ' / \news
mothers ' / ———-
========'/ \the
```

+Explanation+.—The three short horizontal lines represent each a part of the compound subject. They are connected by dotted lines, which stand for the connecting word. The x shows that a conjunction is understood. The line standing for the word modifier is joined to that part of the subject line which represents the entire subject. Turn this diagram about, and the connected horizontal lines will stand for the parts of a compound predicate.

+Oral Analysis+.—*Wives, sisters,* and *mothers* form the compound subject; *anxious* is a modifier of the compound subject; *and* connects *sisters* and *mothers*.

+Parsing+.—*And* is a conjunction connecting *sisters* and *mothers*; *ah* is an interjection, expressing a sudden burst of feeling.

2. In a letter we may advise, exhort, comfort, request, and discuss.

(For diagram see the last sentence of the "Explanation" above.)

3. The mental, moral, and muscular powers are improved by use.

```
         powers came
================== ==========
\The \ X \ and \ \ and \of
    \...\.....\ \.......\ parentage
    \ \ \muscular \ \————————-
     \ \moral \from
      \mental \ land
                   \————————-
```

4. The hero of the Book of Job came from a strange land and of a strange parentage. 5. The optic nerve passes from the brain to the back of the eyeball, and there spreads out. 6. Between the mind of man and the outer world are interposed the nerves of the human body. 7. All forms of the lever and all the principal kinds of hinges are found in the body. 8. By perfection is meant the full and harmonious development of all the faculties. 9. Ugh! I look forward with dread to to-morrow. 10. From the Mount of Olives, the Dead Sea, dark and misty and solemn, is seen. 11. Tush! tush! 't will not again appear. 12. A sort of gunpowder was used at an early period in China and in other parts of Asia. 13. Some men sin deliberately and presumptuously. 14. Feudalism did not and could not exist before the tenth century. 15. The opinions of the New York press are quoted in every port and in every capital. 16. Both friend and foe applauded.

```
      friend
  _____-\
     '\
     '\ | applauded
    'and…. Both >===|===========
     '/
   foe '/
   _____._____/
```

+Explanation+.—The conjunction *both* is used to strengthen the real connective *and*. *Either* and *neither* do the same for *or* and *nor* in *either—or, neither—nor*.

+Remark.+—A phrase that contains another phrase as a modifier is called a
+Complex Phrase+. Two or more phrases connected by a conjunction form

a
+Compound Phrase+.

+Direction.+—*Pick out the simple, the complex, and the compound phrases in the sentences above.*

* * * * *

LESSON 21.

COMPOSITION—CONNECTED TERMS AND INTERJECTIONS.

+COMMA—RULE.—Words or phrases connected by conjunctions are separated from each other by the comma unless all the conjunctions are expressed.+

+Remark+.—When words and phrases stand in pairs, the pairs are separated according to the Rule, but the words of each pair are not.

When one of two terms has a modifier that without the comma might be referred to both, or, when the parts of compound predicates and of other phrases are long or differently modified, these terms or parts are separated by the comma though no conjunction is omitted.

When two terms connected by or have the same meaning, the second is logically explanatory of the first, and is set off by the comma, *i. e.*, when it occurs in the body of a sentence, a comma is placed after the explanatory word, as well as before the *or*.

+Direction.+—*Justify the punctuation of these sentences:*—

1. Long, pious pilgrimages are made to Mecca. 2. Empires rise, flourish, and decay. 3. Cotton is raised in Egypt, in India, and in the United States. 4.

The brain is protected by the skull, or cranium. 5. Nature and art and science were laid under tribute. 6. The room was furnished with a table, and a chair without legs. 7. The old oaken bucket hangs in the well.

+Explanation.+—No comma here, for no conjunction is omitted. *Oaken* limits *bucket, old* limits *bucket* modified by *oaken,* and *the* limits *bucket* modified by *old* and *oaken*. See Lesson 13.

8. A Christian spirit should be shown to Jew or Greek, male or female, friend or foe. 9. We climbed up a mountain for a view.

+Explanation+.—No comma. *Up a mountain* tells where we climbed, and *for a view* tells why we climbed up a mountain.

10. The boy hurries away from home, and enters upon a career of business or
    of pleasure.
11. The long procession was closed by the great dignitaries of the realm,
    and the brothers and sons of the king.

+Direction+.—*Punctuate such of these sentences as need punctuation, and give your reasons*:—

1. Men and women and children stare cry out and run. 2. Bright healthful and vigorous poetry was written by Milton. 3. Few honest industrious men fail of success in life.

(Where is the conjunction omitted?)

4. Ireland or the Emerald Isle lies to the west of England. 5. That relates to the names of animals or of things without sex. 6. The Hebrew is closely allied to the Arabic the Phoenician the Syriac and the Chaldee. 7. We sailed down the river and along the coast and into a little inlet. 8. The horses and

the cattle were fastened in the same stables and were fed with abundance of hay and grain. 9. Spring and summer autumn and winter rush by in quick succession. 10. A few dilapidated old buildings still stand in the deserted village.

+EXCLAMATION POINT—RULE.—All *Exclamatory Expressions* must be followed by the exclamation point.+

+Remark+.—Sometimes an interjection alone and sometimes an interjection and the words following it form the exclamatory expression; as, *Oh! it hurts. Oh, the beautiful snow!*

O is used in direct address; as, *O father, listen to me. Oh* is used as a cry of pain, surprise, delight, fear, or appeal. This distinction, however desirable, is not strictly observed, *O* being frequently used in place of *Oh*.

+CAPITAL LETTERS—RULE.—The words *I* and *O* should be written in capital letters.+

+Direction.+—*Correct these violations of the two rules given above:*—

1. o noble judge o excellent young man. 2. Out of the depths have i cried unto thee. 3. Hurrah the field is won. 4. Pshaw how foolish. 5. Oh oh oh i shall be killed. 6. o life how uncertain o death how inevitable.

* * * * *

LESSON 22.

ANALYSIS AND PARSING.

+Direction+.—*Beginning with the 8th sentence of the first group of exercises in Lesson* 21, *analyze thirteen sentences, omitting the* 4_th *of the* second group._

+Model+.—*A Christian spirit should be shown to Jew or Greek, male or female, friend or foe.*

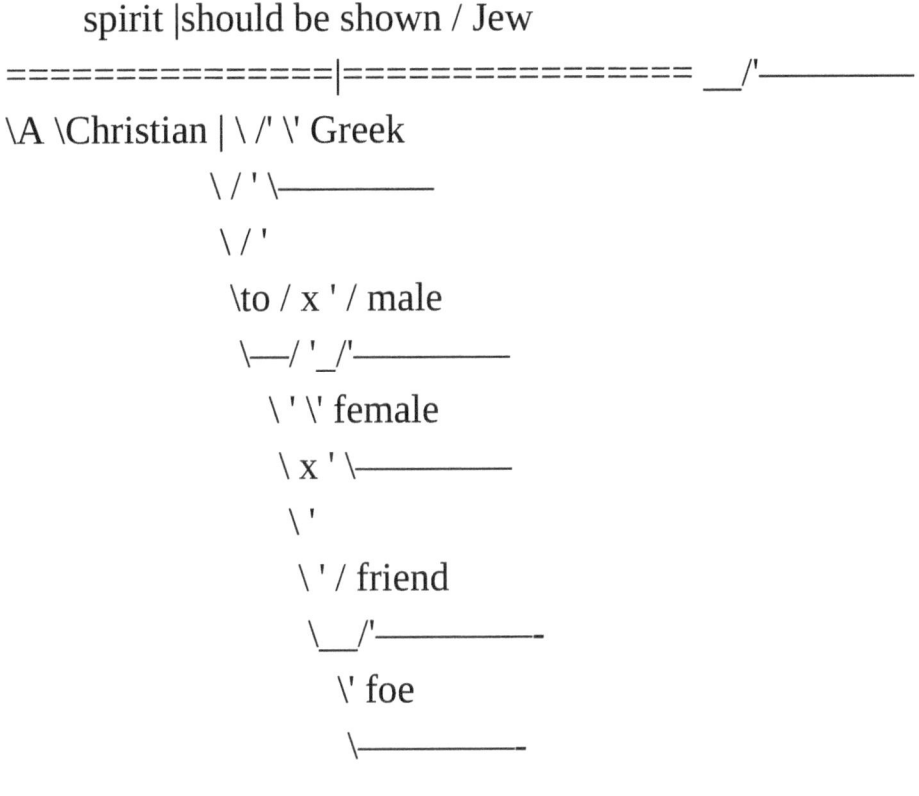

* * * * *

LESSON 23.

COMPOSITION—CONNECTED TERMS.

Direction.+—*Using the nouns below, compose sentences with compound subjects; compose others in which the verbs shall form compound predicates; and others in which the adjectives, the adverbs, and the phrases shall form compound modifiers:—*

In some let there be three or more connected terms. Observe Rule, Lesson 21, for punctuation. Let your sentences mean something.

NOUNS.

Washington, beauty, grace, Jefferson, symmetry, lightning, Lincoln, electricity, copper, silver, flowers, gold, rose, lily.

VERBS.

Examine, sing, pull, push, report, shout, love, hate, like, scream, loathe, approve, fear, obey, refine, hop, elevate, skip, disapprove.

ADJECTIVES.

+Direction.+—*See Caution, Lesson* 13.

Bright, acute, patient, careful, apt, forcible, simple, homely, happy, short, pithy, deep, jolly, mercurial, precipitous.

ADVERBS.

+Direction.+—*See Caution, Lesson 15.* Neatly, slowly, carefully, sadly, now, here, never, hereafter.

PHRASES.

On sea; in the city; by day; on land; by night; in the country; by hook; across the ocean; by crook; over the lands; along the level road; up the mountains.

* * * *

LESSON 24.

REVIEW.

CAPITAL LETTERS AND PUNCTUATION.

Direction.+—*Give the reason for every capital letter and for every mark of punctuation used below:*—

1. The sensitive parts of the body are covered by the cuticle, or skin. 2. The degrees of A.B., A.M., D.D., and LL.D. are conferred by the colleges and the universities of the country. 3. Oh, I am so happy! 4. Fathers and mothers, sons and daughters rejoice at the news. 5. Plants are nourished by the earth, and the carbon of the air. 6. A tide of American travelers is constantly flooding Europe. 7. The tireless, sleepless sun rises above the horizon, and climbs slowly and steadily to the zenith. 8. He retired to private life on half pay, and on the income of a large estate in the South.

+Direction.+—*Write these expressions, using capital letters and marks of punctuation where they belong:*—

1. a fresh ruddy and beardless french youth replied 2. maj, cal, bu, p m, rev, no, hon, ft, w, e, oz, mr, n y, a b, mon, bbl, st 3. o father o father i cannot breathe here 4. ha ha that sounds well 5. the edict of nantes was established by henry the great of france 6. mrs, vs, co, esq, yd, pres, u s, prof, o, do, dr 7. hurrah good news good news 8. the largest fortunes grow by the saving of cents and dimes and dollars 9. the baltic sea lies between sweden and russia 10. the mississippi river pours into the gulf of mexico 11. supt, capt, qt, ph d, p, cr, i e, doz 12. benjamin franklin was born in boston in 1706 and died in 1790

+Direction.+—*Correct all these errors in capitalization and punctuation, and give your reasons:*—

1 Oliver cromwell ruled, over the english People, 2. halloo. I must speak to You! 3. john Milton, went abroad in Early Life, and, stayed, for some time, with the Scholars of Italy, 4. Most Fuel consists of Coal and Wood from the Forests 5. books are read for Pleasure and the Instruction and

improvement of the Intellect, 6. In rainy weather the feet should be protected by overshoes or galoches 7. hark they are coming! 8. A, neat, simple and manly style is pleasing to Us. 9. alas poor thing alas, 10. i fished on a, dark, and cool, and mossy, trout stream.

* * * * *

LESSON 25.

MISCELLANEOUS EXERCISES IN REVIEW.

ANALYSIS.

1. By the streets of By-and-by, one arrives at the house of Never.—*Spanish Proverb* [Footnote: By-and-by has no real streets, the London journals do not actually thunder, nor were the cheeks of William the Testy literally scorched by his fiery gray eyes. *Streets, house, colored, thunder,* and *scorched* are not, then, used here in their first and ordinary meaning, but in a secondary and figurative sense. These words we call +Metaphors+. By what they denote and by what they only suggest they lend clearness, vividness, and force to the thought they help to convey, and add beauty to the expression.

> For further treatment of metaphors and other figures of speech, see pages 87, 136, 155, 156, 165, and Lesson 150.]

2. The winds and waves are always on the side of the ablest navigators.—*Gibbon*.
3. The axis of the earth sticks out visibly through the center of each and every town or city.—*Holmes*.
4. The arrogant Spartan, with a French-like glorification, boasted forever of little Thermopylae.—*De Quincey*.
5. The purest act of knowledge is always colored by some feeling of

pleasure or pain.—*Hamilton.*

6. The thunder of the great London journals reverberates through every clime.—*Marsh.*
7. The cheeks of William the Testy were scorched into a dusky red by two fiery little gray eyes.—*Irving.*
8. The study of natural science goes hand in hand with the culture of the imagination.—*Tyndall.* [Footnote: *Hand in hand* may be treated as one adverb, or *with* may be supplied.]
9. The whole substance of the winds is drenched and bathed and washed and
   winnowed and sifted through and through by this baptism in the sea.—*Swain.*
10. The Arabian Empire stretched from the Atlantic to the Chinese Wall, and
    from the shores of the Caspian Sea to those of the Indian Ocean.—*Draper.*
11. One half of all known materials consists of oxygen.—*Cooke.*
12. The range of thirty pyramids, even in the time of Abraham, looked down
    on the plain of Memphis.—*Stanley.*

* * * * *

LESSON 26.

WRITTEN PARSING.

+Direction+.—*Parse the sentences of Lesson 25 according to this* +Model for Written Parsing.+

| Nouns. | Pron. | Verbs. | Adj. | Adv. | Prep. | Conj.| Int.|

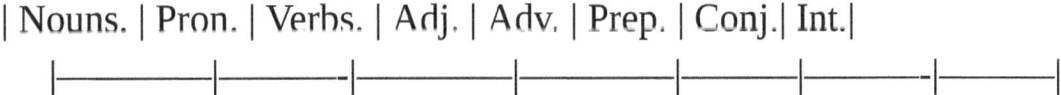

```
            ─|
1st |streets,| | |the,the.| |By,of, | | |
sentence|By-and- | one. |arrives.| | |at,of | | |
        | by, | | | | | | |
        |house, | | | | | | |
        |Never. | | | | | | |
────────|────────|─────|────────|───────|──────|──────|─────|
    ─|
       | | | | | | | |
2d | | | | | | | |
sentence| | | | | | | |
```

TO THE TEACHER.—Until the +Subdivisions+ and +Modifications+ of parts of speech are reached, +Oral and Written Parsing+ can be only a classification of the words in the sentence. You must judge how frequently a lesson like this is needed, and how much parsing should be done orally day by day. In their +Oral Analysis+ let the pupils give at first the reasons for every statement, but guard against their doing this mechanically and in set terms; and, when you think it can safely be done, let them drop it. But ask now and then, whenever you think they have grown careless or are guessing, for the reason of this, that, or the other step taken.

Here it may be well to emphasize the fact that the part of speech to which any word belongs is determined by the use of the word, and not from its form. Such exercises as the following are suggested:—

    Use *right* words.
Act *right*.
Right the wrong.
You are in the *right*.

Pupils will be interested in finding sentences that illustrate the different uses of the same word. It is hardly necessary for us to make lists of words that have different uses. Any dictionary will furnish abundant examples. It is an excellent practice to point out such words in the regular exercises for analysis.

* * * * *

LESSON 27.

REVIEW.

TO THE TEACHER.—See suggestions, Lesson 16.

+Direction+.—*Review from Lesson* 17 *to Lesson* 21, *inclusive*.

Give the substance of the "Introductory Hints" (tell, for example, what such words as *long* and *there* may be expanded into, how these expanded forms may be modified, how introduced, what the introductory words are called, and why, etc.). Repeat and illustrate definitions and rules; illustrate fully what is taught of the position of phrases, and of the punctuation of phrases, connected terms, and exclamatory expressions. How many parts of speech are there?

Exercises on the Composition of the Sentence and the Paragraph.

(SEE PAGES 153-156.)

TO THE TEACHER.—See notes to the teacher, pages 30, 150.

* * * * *

LESSON 28.

NOUNS AS OBJECT COMPLEMENTS.

Introductory Hints.+—In saying *Washington captured*, we do not fully express the act performed by Washington. If we add a noun and say, *Washington captured Cornwallis*, we complete the predicate by naming that which receives the act.

Whatever fills out, or completes, is a +Complement+. As *Cornwallis* completes the expression of the act by naming the thing acted upon—the object—we call it the +Object Complement+. Connected objects completing the same verb form a +Compound Object Complement+; as, Washington captured *Cornwallis* and his *army*.

+DEFINITION.—The *Object Complement of a Sentence* completes the predicate, and names that which receives the act.+

The complement with all its modifiers is called the +Modified Complement.+

+Analysis.+

1. Clear thinking makes clear writing.

```
  thinking | makes | writing
============|=====================
 \ clear |  \clear
```

+Oral Analysis+.—-*Writing* is the object complement; *clear writing* is the modified complement, and *makes clear writing* is the entire predicate.

2. Austerlitz killed Pitt. 3. The invention of gunpowder destroyed feudalism. 4. Liars should have good memories. 5. We find the first

surnames in the tenth century. 6. God tempers the wind to the shorn lamb. 7. Benjamin Franklin invented the lightning-rod. 8. At the opening of the thirteenth century, Oxford took and held rank with the greatest schools of Europe.

```
                took
        /————————-\
Oxford | / ' \ | rank
========|=and' ==========
     | \ ' /
      \ ' held /
       \————-/


           revolves
        /————————
moon | / '
======|== and'
    | \ '
      \ ' keeps | side
       \————————————-
```

9. The moon revolves, and keeps the same side toward us. 10. Hunger rings the bell, and orders up coals in the shape of bread and butter, beef and bacon, pies and puddings. 11. The history of the Trojan war rests on the authority of Homer, and forms the subject of the noblest poem of antiquity. 12. Every stalk, bud, flower, and seed displays a figure, a proportion, a harmony, beyond the reach of art. 13. The natives of Ceylon build houses of the trunk, and thatch roofs with the leaves, of the cocoa-nut palm. 14. Richelieu exiled the mother, oppressed the wife, degraded the brother, and banished the confessor, of the king. 15. James and John study and recite grammar and arithmetic.

```
         James study grammar
=========\ /===========\ /===============
    '\|/'\|/'
   'and ==|== and' ===== and'
John '/|\' recite /\' arithmetic
=========/ \===========/ \===============
```

* * * * *

LESSON 29.

NOUNS AND ADJECTIVES AS ATTRIBUTE COMPLEMENTS.

+Introductory Hints+.—The subject presents one idea; the predicate presents another, and asserts it of the first. *Corn is growing* presents the idea of the thing, corn, and the idea of the act, growing, and asserts the act of the thing. *Corn growing* lacks the asserting word, and *Corn is* lacks the word denoting the idea to be asserted.

In logic, the asserting word is called the *copula*—it shows that the two ideas are coupled into a thought—and the word expressing the idea asserted is called the predicate. But, as one word often performs both offices, e. g., Corn *grows*, and, as it is disputed whether any word can assert without expressing something of the idea asserted, we pass this distinction by as not essential in grammar, and call both that which asserts and that which expresses the idea asserted, by one name—the predicate. [Footnote: We may call the verb the predicate; but, when it is followed by a complement, it is an incomplete predicate.]

The *maple leaves become*. The verb become does not make a complete predicate; it does not fully express the idea to be asserted. The idea may be completely expressed by adding the adjective *red*, denoting the quality we wish to assert of leaves, or attribute to them—*The maple leaves become red.*

Lizards are reptiles. The noun *reptiles*, naming the class of the animals called lizards, performs a like office for the asserting word *are*. *Rolfe's wife was Pocahontas. Pocahontas* completes the predicate by presenting a second idea, which *was* asserts to be identical with that of the subject.

When the completing word expressing the idea to be attributed does not unite with the asserting word to make a single verb, we distinguish it as the +Attribute Complement.+ [Footnote: *Subjective Complement* may, if preferred, be used instead of Attribute Complement.] Connected attribute complements of the same verb form a +Compound Attribute Complement+.

Most grammarians call the adjective and the noun, when so used, the +Predicate Adjective+ and the +Predicate Noun+.

+DEFINITION.—The *Attribute Complement* of a Sentence completes the predicate and belongs to the subject.+

Analysis.

1. Slang is vulgar.

```
 Slang | is \ vulgar
==========|=================
     |
```

+Explanation+.—The line standing for the attribute complement is, like the object line, a continuation of the predicate line; but notice that the line which separates the incomplete predicate from the complement slants toward the subject to show that the complement is an attribute of it.

+Oral Analysis+.—*Vulgar* is the attribute complement, completing the predicate and expressing a quality of slang; *is vulgar* is the entire predicate.

2. The sea is fascinating and treacherous. 3. The mountains are grand, tranquil, and lovable. 4. The Saxon words in English are simple, homely, and substantial. 5. The French and the Latin words in English are elegant, dignified, and artificial. [Footnote: The assertion in this sentence is true only in the main.] 6. The ear is the ever-open gateway of the soul. 7. The verb is the life of the sentence. 8. Good-breeding is surface-Christianity. 9. A dainty plant is the ivy green.

+Explanation+.—The subject names that of which the speaker says something. The terms in which he says it,—the predicate,—he, of course, assumes that the hearer already understands. Settle, then, which—plant or ivy—Dickens supposed the reader to know least about, and which, therefore, Dickens was telling him about; and you settle which word—*plant* or *ivy*—is the subject. (Is it not the writer's poetical conception of "the green ivy" that the reader is supposed not to possess?)

10. The highest outcome of culture is simplicity. 11. Stillness of person and steadiness of features are signal marks of good-breeding. 12. The north wind is full of courage, and puts the stamina of endurance into a man. 13. The west wind is hopeful, and has promise and adventure in it. 14. The east wind is peevishness and mental rheumatism and grumbling, and curls one up in the chimney-corner. 15. The south wind is full of longing and unrest and effeminate suggestions of luxurious ease.

* * * * *

LESSON 30.

ATTRIBUTE COMPLEMENTS—CONTINUED.

Analysis.

1. He went out as mate and came back captain.

```
                as
               ---
                '
        went \ ' mate
       /=====================
 He | / ' \out
====|=and '
   | \ ' came \ captain
       \=====================
            \back
```

+Explanation+.—*Mate,* like *captain,* is an attribute complement. Some would say that the conjunction *as* connects *mate* to *he*; but we think this connection is made through the verb *went,* and that *as* is simply introductory. This is indicated in the diagram.

2. The sun shines bright and hot at midday. 3. Velvet feels smooth, and looks rich and glossy. 4. She grew tall, queenly, and beautiful. 5. Plato and Aristotle are called the two head-springs of all philosophy. 6. Under the Roman law, every son was regarded as a slave. 7. He came a foe and returned a friend. 8. I am here. I am present.

+Explanation+.—The office of an adverb sometimes seems to fade into that of an adjective attribute and is not easily distinguished from it. *Here,* like an adjective, seems to complete *am,* and, like an adverb to modify it. From their form and usual function, *here,* in this example, should be called an adverb, and *present* an adjective.

9. This book is presented to you as a token of esteem and gratitude. 10. The warrior fell back upon the bed a lifeless corpse. 11. The apple tastes and smells delicious. 12. Lord Darnley turned out a dissolute and insolent husband. 13. In the fable of the Discontented Pendulum, the weights hung speechless. 14. The brightness and freedom of the New Learning seemed incarnate in the young and scholarly Sir Thomas More. 15. Sir Philip Sidney lived and died the darling of the Court, and the gentleman and idol of the time.

* * * * *

LESSON 31.

OBJECTIVE COMPLEMENTS.

+Introductory Hints+.—*He made the wall white.* Here *made* does not fully express the act performed upon the wall. We do not mean to say, He *made* the white *wall*, but, He *made-white* (*whitened*) the wall. *White* helps *made* to express the act, and at the same time it denotes the quality attributed to the wall as the result of the act.

They made Victoria queen. Here *made* does not fully express the act performed upon Victoria. They did not *make* Victoria, but *made-queen* (*crowned*) Victoria. *Queen* helps *made* to express the act, and at the same time denotes the office to which the act raised Victoria.

A word that, like the adjective *white* or the noun *queen*, helps to complete the predicate and at the same time belongs to the object complement, differs from an attribute complement by belonging not to the subject but to the object complement, and so is called an +Objective Complement+.

As the objective complement generally denotes what the receiver of the act is made to be, in fact or in thought, it is sometimes called the *factitive complement* or the *factitive object* (Lat. *facere,* to make). [Footnote: See Lesson 37, last foot-note.]

Some of the other verbs which are thus completed are *call, think, choose,* and *name.*

+DEFINITION.—The *Objective Complement* completes the predicate and belongs to the object complement.+

Analysis.

1. They made Victoria queen.

```
They | made / queen | Victoria
======|=========================
   |
```

+Explanation+.—The line that separates *made* from *queen* slants toward the object complement to show that *queen* belongs to the object.

+Oral Analysis+.—*Queen* is an objective complement completing *made* and belonging to *Victoria*; *made Victoria queen* is the complete predicate.

2. Some one has called the eye the window of the soul. 3. Destiny had made Mr. Churchill a schoolmaster. 4. President Hayes chose the Hon. Wm. M. Evarts Secretary of State. 5. After a break of sixty years in the ducal line of the English nobility, James I. created the worthless Villiers Duke of Buckingham. 6. We should consider time as a sacred trust.

+Explanation+.—*As* may be used simply to introduce an objective complement.

7. Ophelia and Polonius thought Hamlet really insane. 8. The President and the Senate appoint certain men ministers to foreign courts. 9. Shylock would have struck Jessica dead beside him. 10. Custom renders the feelings blunt and callous. 11. Socrates styled beauty a short-lived tyranny. 12. Madame de Stael calls beautiful architecture frozen music. 13. They named the state New York from the Duke of York. 14. Henry the Great consecrated the Edict of Nantes as the very ark of the constitution.

* * * * *

LESSON 32.

COMPOSITION—COMPLEMENTS.

+Caution.+—Be careful to distinguish an adjective complement from an adverb modifier.

+Explanation.+—Mary arrived *safe*. We here wish to tell the condition of Mary on her arrival, and not the manner of her arriving. My head feels *bad* (is in a bad condition, as perceived by the sense of feeling). The sun shines *bright* (is bright, as perceived by its shining).

When the idea of being is prominent in the verb, as in the examples above, you see that the adjective, and not the adverb, follows.

+Direction.+—*Justify the use of these adjectives and adverbs:—*

1. The boy is running wild. 2. The boy is running wildly about. 3. They all arrived safe and sound. 4. The day opened bright. 5. He felt awkward in the presence of ladies. 6. He felt around awkwardly for his chair. 7. The sun shines bright. 8. The sun shines brightly on the tree-tops. 9. He appeared prompt and willing. 10. He appeared promptly and willingly.

+Direction+.—*Correct these errors and give your reasons:*—

1. My head pains me very bad. 2. My friend has acted very strange in the matter. 3. Don't speak harsh. 4. It can be bought very cheaply. 5. I feel tolerable well. 6. She looks beautifully.

+Direction+.—*Join to each of the nouns below three appropriate adjectives expressing the qualities as assumed, and then make complete sentences by asserting these qualities:*—

+Model.+ Hard | brittle + glass. transparent |

Glass is hard, brittle, and transparent.

Coal, iron, Niagara Falls, flowers, war, ships.

+Direction+.—*Compose sentences containing these nouns as attribute complements:*—

Emperor, mathematician, Longfellow, Richmond.

+Direction+.—*Compose sentences, using these verbs as predicates, and these pronouns as attribute complements:*—

Is, was, might have been; I, we, he, she, they.

+Remark+.—Notice that these forms of the pronouns—*I, we, thou, he, she, ye, they,* and *who*—are never used as object complements or as principal words in prepositional phrases; and that *me, us, thee, him, her, them,* and *whom* are never used as subjects or as attribute complements of sentences.

+Direction+.—*Compose sentences in which each of the following verbs shall have two complements—the one an object complement, the other an objective complement:*—

Let some object complements be pronouns, and let some objective complements be introduced by *as*.

+Model+.—They call *me chief.* We regard composition *as* very *important.*

Make, appoint, consider, choose, call.

* * * * *

LESSON 33.

NOUNS AS ADJECTIVE MODIFIERS.

+Introductory Hints+.—*Solomon's temple was destroyed.* Solomon's limits *temple* by telling what or whose temple is spoken of, and is therefore a modifier of *temple*.

The relation of Solomon to the temple is expressed by the apostrophe and *s* ('s) added to the noun *Solomon*. When *s* has been added to the noun to denote more than one, this relation of possession is expressed by the apostrophe alone ('); as, *boys'* hats. This same relation of possession may be expressed by the preposition *of; Solomon's* temple = the temple *of Solomon.*

Dom Pedro, the emperor, was welcomed by the Americans. The noun *emperor* modifies *Dom Pedro* by telling what Dom Pedro is meant. Both words name the same person.

Solomon's and *emperor*, like adjectives, modify nouns; but they are names of things, and are modified by adjectives and not by adverbs; as, *the wise* Solomon's temple; Dom Pedro, *the Brazilian* emperor. These are conclusive reasons for calling such words nouns.

They represent two kinds of +Noun Modifiers+—the +Possessive+ and the
+Explanatory+.

The Explanatory Modifier is often called an +Appositive+. It identifies or explains by adding another name of the same thing.

Analysis.

1. Elizabeth's favorite, Raleigh, was beheaded by James I.

```
    favorite (Raleigh) | was beheaded
====================|==============
\Elizabeth's | \by
              \ James I
               \——————-
```

+Oral Analysts+.—*Elizabeth's* and *Raleigh* are modifiers of the subject; the first word telling whose favorite is meant, the second what favorite. *Elizabeth's favorite, Raleigh* is the modified subject.

2. The best features of King James's translation of the Bible are derived from Tyndale's version. 3. St. Paul, the apostle, was beheaded in the reign of Nero. 4. A fool's bolt is soon shot. 5. The tadpole, or polliwog, becomes a frog. 6. An idle brain is the devil's workshop. 7. Mahomet, or Mohammed, was born in the year 569 and died in 632. 8. They scaled Mount Blanc—a daring feat.

```
   They | scaled | Mount Blanc ( feat )
======|====================== =======
```

| \a \daring

+Explanation+.—*Feat* is explanatory of the sentence, *They scaled Mount Blanc,* and in the diagram it stands, enclosed in curves, on a short line placed after the sentence line.

9. Bees communicate to each other the death of the queen, by a rapid interlacing of the antennae. [Footnote: For uses of *each other* and *one another,* see Lesson 124.]

+Explanation+.—*Each other* may be treated as one term, or *each* may be made explanatory of *bees.*

10. The lamp of a man's life has three wicks—brain, blood, and breath.

+Explanation.+—Several words may together be explanatory of one.

11. The turtle's back-bone and breast-bone—its shell and coat of armor—are on the outside of its body.

```
       back-bone    shell
=============\  ========\
      '\ /' \ | are
    and' \==========(======/ 'and \=)=|=======
      ' / \turtle's \its \ ' / |
breast-bone '/ \The \' coat /
=============/  ========/
```

12. Cromwell's rule as Protector began in the year 1653 and ended in 1658.

+Explanation+.—*As, namely, to wit, viz., i.e., e.g.,* and *that is* may introduce explanatory modifiers, but they do not seem to connect them to the words modified. In the diagram they stand like *as* in Lesson 30. *Protector* is explanatory of *Cromwell's*.

13. In the latter half of the eighteenth century, three powerful nations, namely, Russia, Austria, and Prussia, united for the dismemberment of Poland.
14. John, the beloved disciple, lay on his Master's breast.
15. The petals of the daisy, *day's-eye,* close at night and in rainy weather.

* * * * *

LESSON 34.

COMPOSITION—NOUNS AS ADJECTIVE MODIFIERS.

+COMMA—RULE.—An *Explanatory Modifier*, when it does not restrict the modified term or combine closely with it, is set off by the comma.+ [Footnote: See foot-note, Lesson 18]

+Explanation+.—*The words I and O should be written in capital letters.* The phrase *I and O* restricts *words*, that is, limits its application, and no comma is needed.

Jacob's favorite sons, Joseph and Benjamin, were Rachel's children. The phrase *Joseph and Benjamin* explains sons without restricting, and therefore should be set off by the comma.

In each of these expressions, *I myself, we boys, William the Conqueror,* the explanatory term combines closely with the word explained, and no comma is needed.

* * * * *

LESSON 36.

REVIEW.

TO THE TEACHER.—See suggestions, Lesson 16.

+Direction.+—*Review from Lesson 28 to Lesson 35, inclusive.*

Give the substance of the "Introductory Hints" (for example, show clearly what two things are essential to a complete predicate; explain what is meant by a complement; distinguish clearly the three kinds of complements; show what parts of speech may be employed for each, and tell what general idea—action, quality, class, or identity—is expressed by each attribute complement or objective complement in your illustrations, etc.). Repeat and illustrate definitions and rules; explain and illustrate fully the distinction between an adjective complement and an adverb modifier; illustrate what is taught of the forms *I*, *we*, etc., *me*, *us*, etc.; explain and illustrate the use of the possessive sign.

Exercises on the Composition of the Sentence and the Paragraph.

(SEE PAGES 156-159.)

TO THE TEACHER.—See suggestions to the teacher, pages 30, 150.

* * * * *

LESSON 37.

VERBS AS ADJECTIVES AND AS NOUNS—PARTICIPLES.

+Introductory Hints.+—*Corn grows; Corn growing.* Here *growing* differs from *grows* in lacking the power to assert. *Growing* is a form of the verb that cannot, like *grows*, make a complete predicate because it only assumes or implies that the corn does the act. *Corn* may be called the assumed subject of *growing.*

Birds, singing, delight us. Here *singing* does duty (1) as an adjective, describing birds by assuming or implying an act, and (2) as a verb by expressing the act of singing as going on at the time birds delight us.

By singing their songs birds delight us. Here *singing* has the nature of a verb and that of a noun. As a verb it has an object complement, *songs*; and as a noun it names the act, and stands as the principal word in a prepositional phrase.

Their singing so sweetly delights us. Here, also, *singing* has the nature of a verb and that of a noun. As a verb it has an adverb modifier, *sweetly*, and as a noun it names an act and takes a possessive modifier.

This form of the verb is called the +Participle+ (Lat. *pars*, a part, and *capere*, to take) because it partakes of two natures and performs two offices—those of a verb and an adjective, or those of a verb and a noun. (For definition see Lesson 131.)

Singing birds delight us. Here *singing* has lost its verbal nature, and expresses a permanent quality of birds—telling what kind of birds,—and consequently is a mere adjective. *The singing of the birds delights us.* Here *singing* is simply a noun, naming the act and taking adjective modifiers.

There are two kinds of participles; [Footnote: Grammarians are not agreed as to what these words that have the nature of the verb and that of the noun should be called. Some would call the simple forms *doing, writing*, and *injuring*, in sentences (1), (6), and (7), Lesson 38, *Infinitives*. They would also call by the same name such compound forms as *being accepted, having been shown*, and *having said* in these expressions: "for the purpose of being accepted;" "is the having been shown over a place;" "I recollect his having said that." But does it not tax even credulity to believe that a simple Anglo-Saxon infinitive in *-an*, only one form of which followed a preposition, and that always *to*, could have developed into many compound forms, used in both voices, following almost any preposition, and modified by *the* and by nouns and pronouns in the possessive? No wonder the grammarian Mason says, "An infinitive in *-ing*, set down by some as a modification of the simple infinitive in *-an* or *-en*, is a perfectly unwarranted invention."

Others call these words modernized forms of the Anglo-Saxon *Verbal Nouns* in *-ung, -ing*. But this derivation of them encounters the stubborn fact that those verbal nouns never were compound, and never were or could be followed by objects. These words, on the contrary, are compound, as we have seen, and have objects. That they are from nouns in *-ung* is otherwise, and almost for the same reasons, as incredible as that they are from infinitives in *-an*.

Others call these words *Gerunds*. A gerund in Latin is a simple form of the verb in the active voice, never found in the nominative, and never in the accusative (objective) after a verb. A gerund in Anglo-Saxon is a simple form of the verb in the active voice—the dative case of the infinitive merely—used mainly to indicate purpose, and always preceded by the preposition *to*. To call these words in question gerunds is to stretch the term *gerund* immensely beyond its meaning in Anglo-Saxon, and make it cover words which sometimes (1) are highly compounded; sometimes (2) are used in the passive voice; sometimes (3) follow other prepositions than *to*; sometimes (4) do not follow any preposition; sometimes (5) are objects of verbs;

sometimes (6) are subjects of verbs; sometimes (7) are modified by *the*; sometimes (8) are modified by a noun or pronoun in the possessive; and generally (9) do not indicate purpose. We submit that the extension of a class term so as to include words having these relations that the Anglo-Saxon gerund never had, is not warranted by any precedent except that furnished above in the extension of the term *infinitive* or of the term *verbal noun*!

Still others call some of these words *Infinitives*; some of them *Verbal Nouns*; and some of them *Gerunds*.

The forms in question—*seeing, having seen, being seen, having been seen*, and *having been seeing*, for instance—are now made from the verb in precisely the same way when partaking the nature of the noun as when partaking the nature of the adjective. What can they possibly be but the forms that all grammarians call *participles* extended to new uses? If the uses of the original participles have been extended, why may we not carry over the name? The name *participle* is as true to its etymology when applied to the nounal use of the verb as when applied to the adjectival use. For convenience of classification we call these disputed forms *participles*, as good grammarians long ago called them and still call them, though some of them may be traced back to the Saxon verbal noun or to the infinitive, and though the Saxon participle was adjectival. The name *participle* neither confounds terms nor misleads the student. The nounal and the adjectival uses of participial forms we distinguish very sharply.] one sharing the nature of the verb and that of the adjective; the other, the nature of the verb and that of the noun. Participles commonly end in *ing, ed*, or *en*.

The participle, like other forms of the verb, may be followed by an object complement or an attribute complement.

Analysis and Parsing.

The +participle+ may be used as an +adjective modifier+.

1. Hearing a step, I turned.

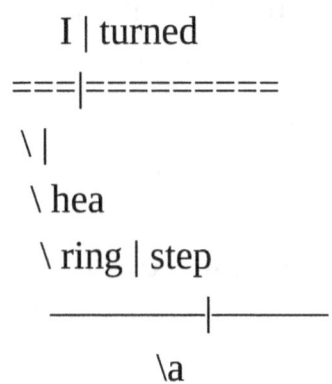

+Explanation+.—The line standing for the participle is broken; one part slants to represent the adjective nature of the participle, and the other is horizontal to represent its verbal nature.

+Oral Analysis+.—The phrase *hearing a step* is a modifier of the subject; [Footnote: Logically, or in sense, *hearing a step* modifies the predicate also. I *turned when* or *because* I heard a step. See Lesson 79.] the principal word is *hearing*, which is completed by the noun *step*; *step* is modified by *a*.

+Parsing+.—*Hearing* is a form of the verb called participle because the act expressed by it is merely assumed, and it shares the nature of an adjective and that of a verb.

2. The fat of the body is fuel laid away for use.

+Explanation+.—The complement is here modified by a participle phrase.

3. The spinal marrow, proceeding from the brain, extends down-ward through
the back-bone.

4. Van Twiller sat in a huge chair of solid oak, hewn in the celebrated forest of the Hague.

+Explanation+.—The principal word of a prepositional phrase is here modified by a participle phrase.

5. Lentulus, returning with victorious legions, had amused the populace with the sports of the amphitheater.

The +participle+ may be used as an +attribute complement+.

6. The natives came crowding around.

+Explanation+.—*Crowding* here completes the predicate *came*, and belongs to the subject *natives*. The natives are represented as performing the act of coming and the accompanying act of crowding. The assertive force of the predicate *came* seems to extend over both verbs. [Footnote: Some grammarians prefer to treat the participle in such constructions as adverbial. But is *crowding* any more adverbial here than are *pale* and *trembling* in "The natives came *pale* and *trembling*"?]

7. The city lies sleeping. 8. They stood terrified. 9. The philosopher sat buried in thought.

```
       \and \and \
     \....\....\
      \ \ \star
       \ \ \ ving
        \ \sav \————-
         \ \ ing
          \gru \————
           \ bbing
```

```
            \——————-
             |
miser | kept \ / \
======|=====================
      |
```

10. The old miser kept grubbing and saving and starving.

The +participle+ may be used as an +objective complement+.

11. He kept me waiting.

+Explanation+.—*Waiting* completes *kept* and relates to the object complement *me*. *Kept-waiting* expresses the complete act performed upon me. *He kept-waiting me=He detained me*. The relation of *waiting* to *me* may be seen by changing the form of the verb; as, I *was kept waiting*. See Lesson 31.

12. I found my book growing dull. [Footnote: It will be seen by this and following examples that we extend the application of the term *objective complement* beyond its primary, or factitive, sense. In "I struck the man *dead*," the condition expressed by *dead* is the result of the act expressed by *struck*. In "I found the man *dead*," the condition is not the result of the act, and so grammarians say that in this second example *dead* should be treated simply as an "appositive" adjective modifying *man*. While *dead* does not belong to *man* as expressing the result of the act, it is made to belong to *man* through the asserting force of the verb, and therefore is not a mere modifier of *man*. *Dead* helps *found* to express the act. Not *found*, but *found-dead* tells what was done to the man.

If we put the sentence in the passive form, "The man was found *dead*," it will be seen that *dead* is more than a mere modifier; it belongs to *man* through the assertive force of *was found*. If *dead* is here merely an "appositive" adjective, "I found the man dead" must equal "I found the man, who was dead" (or, "and he was dead"). The two sentences obviously are not equal. "I caught him asleep" does not mean, "I caught him, and he was asleep."

If, in the construction discussed above, *dead* is an objective complement, *quiet*, *stirring*, and (to) *stir* in the following sentences are objective complements:—

    I saw the leaves quiet.
I saw the leaves stirring.
I saw the leaves stir.

The adjective, the participle, and the infinitive do not here seem to differ essentially in office. See Lesson 31 and page 78.]

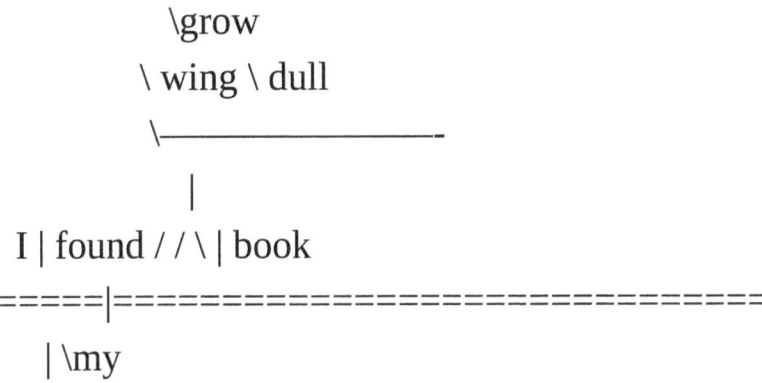

+Explanation+.—The diagram representing the phrase complement is drawn above the complement line, on which it is made to rest by means of a support. All that stands on the complement line is regarded as the complement. Notice that the little mark before the phrase points toward the object complement. The adjective *dull* completes *growing* and belongs to *book*, the assumed subject of *growing*.

13. He owned himself defeated. 14. No one ever saw fat men heading a riot or herding together in turbulent mobs. 15. I felt my heart beating faster. 16. You may imagine me sitting there. 17. Saul, seeking his father's asses, found himself suddenly turned into a king.

* * * * *

LESSON 38.

PARTICIPLES—CONTINUED.

Analysis and Parsing.

The +participle+ may be used as +principal word+ in a +prepositional phrase+.

1. We receive good by doing good.

```
   We | receive | good
=====|====================
   | \by
       \——-,doing | good
       _____
```

+Explanation+.—The line representing the participle here is broken; the first part represents the participle as a noun, and the other as a verb.

+Oral Analysis+.—The phrase *by doing good* is a modifier of the predicate; *by* introduces the phrase; the principal word is *doing*, which is completed by the noun *good*.

+Passing+.—*Doing* is a participle; like a noun, it follows the preposition *by*, and, like a verb, it takes an object complement.

2. Portions of the brain may be cut off without producing any pain. 3. The Coliseum was once capable of seating ninety thousand persons. 4. Success generally depends on acting prudently, steadily, and vigorously. 5. You cannot fully sympathize with suffering without having suffered. (*Suffering* is here a noun.)

The +participle+ may be the +principal word+ in a phrase used as a +subject+ or as an +object complement+.

6. Your writing that letter so neatly secured the position.

```
—-, writing | letter
'_____

 \Your | \neatly \that
      | \so
      |
      / \ | secured | position
    =========|=========='===========
         | \the
```

+Explanation+.—The diagram of the subject phrase is drawn above the subject line. All that rests on the subject line is regarded as the subject.

+Oral Analysis+.—The phrase *your writing that letter so neatly* is the subject; the principal word of it is *writing*, which is completed by *letter; writing*, as a noun, is modified by *your*, and, as a verb, by the adverb phrase *so neatly*.

7. We should avoid injuring the feelings of others. 8. My going there will depend upon my father's giving his consent. 9. Good reading aloud is a rare accomplishment.

The +participial form+ may be used as a +mere noun+ or a +mere adjective+.

10. The cackling of geese saved Rome.

11. Such was the exciting campaign, celebrated in many a long-forgotten song. [Footnote: "*Manig man* in Anglo-Saxon was used like German *mancher mann*, Latin *multus vir*, and the like, until the thirteenth century; when the article was inserted to emphasize the distribution before indicated by the singular number."—*Prof. F. A. March.*]

+Explanation+.—*Many* modifies *song* after *song* has been limited by *a* and *long-forgotten*.

12. All silencing of discussion is an assumption of infallibility. 13. He was a squeezing, grasping, hardened old sinner.

The +participle+ may be used in +independent+ or +absolute phrases+.

14. The bridge at Ashtabula giving way, the train fell into the river.

+Explanation+.—The diagram of the absolute phrase, which consists of a noun used independently with a participle, stands by itself. See lesson 44.

15. Talking of exercise, you have heard, of course, of Dickens's "constitutionals."

* * * * *

LESSON 39.

COMPOSITION—PARTICIPLES.

+COMMA—RULE.—The Participle used as an adjective modifier, with the words belonging to it, is set off+ [Footnote: An expression in the body of a sentence is set off by two commas; at the beginning or at the end, by one comma.] +by the comma unless restrictive+.

+Explanation+.—*A bird, lighting near my window, greeted me with a song. The bird sitting on the wall is a wren. Lighting* describes without restricting; *sitting* restricts—limits the application of *bird* to a particular bird.

+Direction+.—*Justify the punctuation of the participle phrases in Lesson 37.*

+Caution+.—In using a participle, be careful to leave no doubt as to what you intend it to modify.

+Direction+.—*Correct these errors in arrangement, and punctuate, giving your reasons:—*

1. A gentleman will let his house going abroad for the summer to a small family containing all the improvements.
2. The town contains fifty houses and one hundred inhabitants built of brick.
3. Suits ready made of material cut by an experienced tailor handsomely trimmed and bought at a bargain are offered cheap.
4. Seated on the topmost branch of a tall tree busily engaged in gnawing an acorn we espied a squirrel.
5. A poor child was found in the streets by a wealthy and benevolent gentleman suffering from cold and hunger.

+Direction+.—*Recast these sentences, making the reference of the participle clear, and punctuating correctly:—*

+Model+.—*Climbing to the top of the hill the Atlantic ocean was seen.* Incorrect because it appears that the ocean did the climbing.

Climbing to the top of the hill, we saw the Atlantic ocean.

1. Entering the next room was seen a marble statue of Apollo. 2. By giving him a few hints he was prepared to do the work well. 3. Desiring an early start the horse was saddled by five o'clock.

+Direction+.—*Compose sentences in which each of these three participles shall be used as an adjective modifier, as the principal word in a prepositional phrase, as the principal word in a phrase used as a subject or as an object complement, as a mere adjective, as a mere noun, and in an absolute phrase:—*

Buzzing, leaping, waving.

* * * * *

LESSON 40.

VERBS AS NOUNS—INFINITIVES.

+Introductory Hints+.—*I came to see you.* Here the verb *see*, like the participle, lacks asserting power—*I to see* asserts nothing. *See*, following the preposition *to*, [Footnote: For the discussion of *to* with the infinitive, see Lesson 134.] names the act and is completed by *you*, and so does duty as a noun and as a verb. In office it is like the second kind of participles, described in Lesson 37, and from many grammarians has received the same name—some calling both *gerunds,* and others calling both *infinitives*. It differs from this participle in form, and in following only the preposition *to*. Came *to see*=came *for seeing*.

This form of the verb is frequently the principal word of a phrase used as a subject or as an object, complement; as, *To read good books* is profitable; I like *to read good books*. Here also the form with *to* is equivalent to the participle form *reading*. *Reading good books* is profitable.

As this form of the verb names the action in an indefinite way, without limiting it to a subject, we call it the +Infinitive+ (Lat. *infinitus*, without limit). For definition, see Lesson 131. The infinitive, like the participle, may have what is called an *assumed subject*. The *assumed subject* denotes that to which the action or being expressed by the participle or the infinitive belongs.

Frequently the infinitive phrase expresses purpose, as in the first example given above, and in such cases *to* expresses relation, and performs its full function as a preposition; but, when the infinitive phrase is used as subject or as object complement, the *to* expresses no relation. It serves only to introduce the phrase, and in no way affects the meaning of the verb.

The infinitive, like other forms of the verb, may be followed by the different complements.

Analysis and Parsing.

The +infinitive phrase+ may be used as an +adjective modifier+ or an +adverb modifier+.

1. The hot-house is a trap to catch sunbeams.

```
  hot-house | is \ trap
============|================
  \The |     \a \to
```

```
\ catch | sunbeams
 _____._____
```

+Oral Analysis+.—*To* introduces the phrase; *catch* is the principal word, and *sunbeams* completes it.

+Parsing+.—*To* is a preposition, introducing the phrase and showing the relation, in sense, of the principal word to *trap; catch* is a form of the verb called *infinitive*; like a noun, it follows the preposition *to* and names the action, and, like a verb, it is completed by *sunbeams*.

2. Richelieu's title to command rested on sublime force of will and decision of character. 3. Many of the attempts to assassinate William the Silent were defeated. 4. We will strive to please you.

+Explanation+.—The infinitive phrase is here used adverbially to modify the predicate.

5. Ingenious Art steps forth to fashion and refine the race. 6. These harmless delusions tend to make us happy.

+Explanation+.—*Happy* completes *make* and relates to *us*.

7. Wounds made by words are hard to heal.

+Explanation+.—The infinitive phrase is here used adverbially to modify the adjective *hard*. *To heal = to be healed*.

8. The representative Yankee, selling his farm, wanders away to seek new lands, to clear new cornfields, to build another shingle palace, and again to sell off and wander.
9. These apples are not ripe enough to eat.

+Explanation+.—The infinitive phrase is here used adverbially to modify the adverb *enough*. *To eat = to be eaten.*

The +infinitive phrase+ may be used as +subject+ or +complement.+

10. To be good is to be great.

```
  \To           \to
\ be \good \ be \ great
 \————————————-
   ||
   / \ | is \ / \
========|==================
    |
```

Explanation.—*To*, in each of these phrases, shows no relation—it serves merely to introduce. The complements *good* and *great* are adjectives used abstractly, having no noun to relate to.

11. To bear our fate is to conquer it. 12. To be entirely just in our estimate of others is impossible. 13. The noblest vengeance is to forgive. 14. He seemed to be innocent.

+Explanation+.—The infinitive phrase here performs the office of an adjective. *To be innocent = innocent.*

15. The blind men's dogs appeared to know him. 16. We should learn to govern ourselves.

+Explanation+.—The infinitive phrase is here used as an object complement.

17. Each hill attempts to ape her voice.

* * * * *

LESSON 41.

INFINITIVES—CONTINUED.

Analysis.

The +infinitive phrase+ may be used +after a preposition+ as the +principal term+ of another phrase.

1. My friend is about to leave me.

```
            \to
         \ leave | me
          _____.____
      \ about |
       \ / \
          _____-
           |
 friend | is \ / \
========|====================
   \My |
```

+Explanation+.—The preposition *about* introduces the phrase used as attribute complement; the principal part is the infinitive phrase *to leave me*.

2. Paul was now about to open his mouth. 3. No way remains but to go on.

+Explanation+.—*But* is here a preposition.

The +infinitive+ and its +assumed subject+ may form the +principal term+ in a phrase introduced by the preposition +for+.

4. For us to know our faults is profitable.

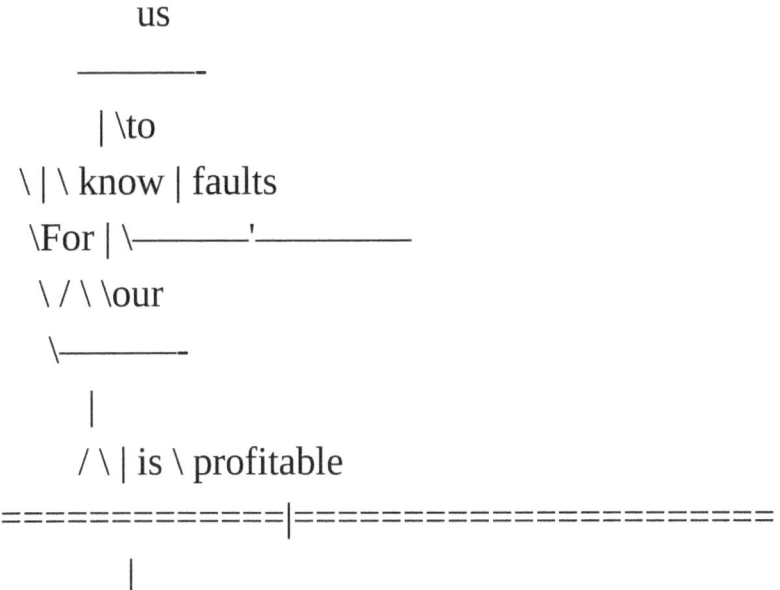

+Explanation+.—*For* introduces the subject phrase; the principal part of the entire phrase is *us to know our faults;* the principal word is *us*, which is modified by the phrase *to know our faults*.

5. God never made his work for man to mend.

+Explanation+.—-The principal term of the phrase *for man to mend* is not *man*, but *man to mend*.

6. For a man to be proud of his learning is the greatest ignorance.

The +infinitive phrase+ may be used as an +explanatory modifier.+

7. It is easy to find fault.

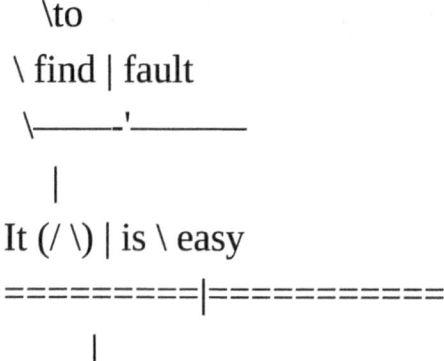

+Explanation+.—The infinitive phrase *to find fault* explains the subject *it*. Read the sentence without *it*, and you will see the real nature of the phrase. This use of *it* as a substitute for the real subject is a very common idiom of our language. It allows the real subject to follow the verb, and thus gives the sentence balance of parts.

8. It is not the way to argue down a vice to tell lies about it. 9. It is natural to man to indulge in the illusions of hope. 10. It is not all of life to live. 11. This task, to teach the young, may become delightful.

The +infinitive phrase+ may be used as +objective complement.+

12. He made me wait.

+Explanation+.—The infinitive *wait* (here used without *to*) completes *made* and relates to *me*. He made-wait me = He detained me.

See "Introductory Hints," Lesson 31, and participles used as objective complements, Lesson 37. Compare *I saw him do it* with *I saw him doing it*. Compare also *He made the stick bend*—equaling *He made-bend* (= bent) *the stick*—with *He made the stick straight*—equaling *He made-straight* (= straightened) *the stick*.

The relation of these objective complements to *me, him,* and *stick* may be more clearly seen by changing the form of the verb, thus: I was made *to wait*; He was seen *to do it*, He was seen *doing it*; The stick was made *to bend*; The stick was made *straight*.

13. We found the report to be true. [Footnote: Some prefer to treat *the report to be true* as an object clause because it is equivalent to the clause *that the report is true*. But many expressions logically equivalent are entirely different in grammatical construction; as, I desire *his promotion*; I desire *him to be promoted*; I desire *that he should be promoted*. Besides, to teach that *him* is the subject, and *to be promoted* the predicate, of a clause would certainly be confusing.]

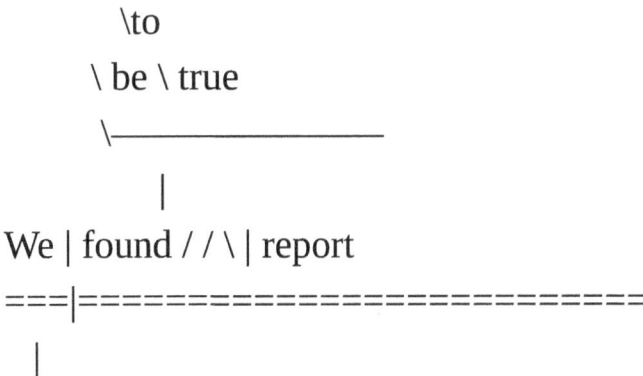

14. He commanded the bridge to be lowered. [Footnote: Notice the difference in construction between this sentence and the sentence *He commanded him to lower the bridge. Him* represents the one to whom the command is given, and *to lower the bridge* is the object complement. This last sentence = He commanded *him that he should lower the bridge.* Compare *He told me to go* with *He told (to) me a story*; also *He taught me to read* with *He taught (to) me reading.* In such sentences as (13) and (14) it may not always be expedient to demand that the pupil shall trace the exact relations of the infinitive phrase to the preceding noun and to the predicate verb. If preferred, in such cases, the infinitive and its assumed subject may

be treated as a kind of phrase object, equivalent to a clause. This construction is similar to the Latin "accusative with the infinitive."]

15. I saw the leaves stir. [Footnote: See pages 68 and 69, foot-note.]

+Explanation+.—*Stir* is an infinitive without the *to*.

16. Being persuaded by Poppaesa, Hero caused his mother, Agrippina, to be assassinated.

* * * * *

LESSON 42.

INFINITIVES—CONTINUED.

Analysis.

The +infinitive phrase+ may be used +independently+. [Footnote: These infinitive phrases can be expanded into dependent clauses. See Lesson 79.

For the infinitive after *as, than*, etc., see Lesson 63. Participles and infinitives unite with other verbs to make compound forms; as, have *walked*, shall *walk*.]

+Explanation+.—In the diagram the independent element must stand by itself.

1. England's debt, to put it in round numbers, is $4,000,000,000. 2. Every object has several faces, so to speak. 3. To make a long story short, Louis XVI. and Marie Antoinette were executed.

Infinitives and Participles.

MISCELLANEOUS.

4. It is a good thing to give thanks unto the Lord. 5. We require clothing in the summer to protect the body from the heat of the sun. 6. Rip Van Winkle could not account for everything's having changed so. 7. This sentence is not too difficult for me to analyze. 8. The fog came pouring in at every chink and keyhole, 9. Conscience, her first law broken, wounded lies. 10. To be, or not to be,—that is the question. 11. I supposed him to be a gentleman. 12. Food, keeping the body in health by making it warm and repairing its waste, is a necessity. 13. I will teach you the trick to prevent your being cheated another time. 14. She threatened to go beyond the sea, to throw herself out of the window, to drown herself. 15. Busied with public affairs, the council would sit for hours smoking and watching the smoke curl from their pipes to the ceiling.

* * * * *

LESSON 43.

COMPOSITION—THE INFINITIVE.

+Direction+.—*Change the infinitives in these sentences into participles, and the participles into infinitives:*—

Notice that *to*, the only preposition used with the infinitive, is changed to *toward, for, of, at, in,* or *on,* when the infinitive is changed to a participle.

1. I am inclined to believe it. 2. I am ashamed to be seen there. 3. She will be grieved to hear it. 4. They trembled to hear such words. 5. It will serve for amusing the children. 6. There is a time to laugh. 7. I rejoice to hear it. 8. You are prompt to obey. 9. They delight to do it. 10. I am surprised at seeing you. 11. Stones are used in ballasting vessels.

+Direction+.—*Improve these sentences by changing the participles into infinitives, and the infinitives into participles:*—

1. We began ascending the mountain. 2. He did not recollect to have paid it. 3. I commenced to write a letter. 4. It is inconvenient being poor. 5. It is not wise complaining.

+Direction+.—*Vary these sentences as in the model:—*

+Model+.—*Rising early* is healthful; *To rise* early is healthful; *It* is healthful *to rise* early; *For one to rise* early is healthful.

(Notice that the explanatory phrase after *it* is not set off by the comma.)

1. Reading good books is profitable. 2. Equivocating is disgraceful. 3. Slandering is base. 4. Indorsing another's paper is dangerous. 5. Swearing is sinful.

+Direction.+—*Write nine sentences, in three of which the infinitive phrase shall be used as an adjective, in three as an adverb, and in three as a noun.*

+Direction.+—*Write eight sentences in which these verbs shall be followed by an infinitive without the to:—*

+Model.+—We *saw* the sun *sink* behind the mountain.

Bid, dare, feel, hear, let, make, need, and see.

* * * * *

LESSON 44.

WORDS AND PHRASES USED INDEPENDENTLY.

+Introductory Hints.+—In this Lesson we wish to notice words and phrases that in certain uses have no grammatical connection with the rest of the sentence.

The fault, dear Brutus, is not in our stars. *Dear Brutus* serves only to arrest attention, and is independent by address.

Poor man! he never came back again. *Poor man* is independent by exclamation.

Thy rod and thy staff, they comfort me. *Rod* and *staff* simply call attention to the objects before anything is said of them, and are independent by pleonasm—a construction used sometimes for rhetorical effect, but out of place in ordinary speech.

His master being absent, the business was neglected. *His master being absent* logically modifies the verb *was neglected* by assigning the cause, but the phrase has no connective expressed or understood, and is therefore grammatically independent. This is called the *absolute phrase.* An *absolute phrase* consists of a noun or a pronoun used independently with a modifying participle.

His conduct, generally speaking, was honorable. *Speaking* is a participle without connection, and with the adverb *generally* forms an independent phrase.

To confess the truth, I was wrong. The infinitive phrase is independent.

The adverbs *well, now, why, there* are sometimes independent; as, *Well*, life is an enigma; *Now*, that is strange; *Why*, it is already noon; *There* are pitch-pine Yankees and white-pine Yankees.

Interjections are without grammatical connection, as you have learned, and hence are independent.

Whatever is enclosed within marks of parenthesis is also independent of the rest of the sentence; as, I stake my fame (*and I had fame*), my heart, my hope, my soul, upon this cast.

+Analysis+.

1. The loveliest things in life, Tom, are but shadows.

+Explanation.+—*Tom* is independent by address. *But* is an adjective modifying *shadows*.

2. There are one-story intellects, two-story intellects, and three-story intellects with skylights.

+Explanation+.—Often, as in this sentence, *there* is used idiomatically, merely to throw the subject after the verb, the idea of place having faded out of the word. To express place, another *there* may follow the predicate; as, *There* is gold *there*.

3. Ah! then and there was hurrying to and fro. 4. Hope lost, all is lost. 5. The smith, a mighty man is he. 6. Why, this is not revenge. 7. Well, this is the forest of Arden. 8. Now, there is at Jerusalem, by the sheep-market, a pool. 9. To speak plainly, your habits are your worst enemies. 10. No accident occurring, we shall arrive to-morrow. 11. The teacher being sick, there was no school Friday. 12. Mr. President, I shall enter on no encomium upon Massachusetts. 13. Properly speaking, there can be no chance in our affairs. 14. But the enemies of tyranny—their path leads to the scaffold. 15. She (oh, the artfulness of the woman!) managed the matter extremely well.

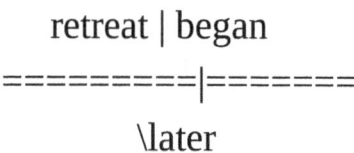

```
    \—-\
     \ day
      \————-
          \A
```

16. A day later (Oct. 19, 1812) began the fatal retreat of the Grand Army, from Moscow.

See Lesson 35.

* * * * *

LESSON 45.

COMPOSITION—INDEPENDENT WORDS AND PHRASES.

+COMMA—RULE.—Words and phrases independent or nearly so are set off by the comma.+

+Remark+.—Interjections, as you have seen, are usually followed by the exclamation point; and *there*, used merely to introduce, is never set off by the comma. When the break after pleonastic expressions is slight, as in (5), Lesson 44, the comma is used; but, if it is more abrupt, as in (14), the dash is required. If the independent expression can be omitted without affecting the sense, it may be enclosed within marks of parenthesis, as in (15) and (16). (For the uses of the dash and the marks of parenthesis, see Lesson 148.)

Words and phrases nearly independent are those which, like *however, of course, indeed, in short, by the bye, for instance,* and *accordingly*, do not modify a word or a phrase alone, but rather the sentence as a whole; as, Lee did not, *however*, follow Washington's orders.

+Direction.+—*Write sentences illustrating the several kinds of independent expressions, and punctuate according to the Rule as explained.*

+Direction.+—*Write short sentences in which these words and phrases, used in a manner nearly independent, shall occur, and punctuate them properly*:—

In short, indeed, now and then, for instance, accordingly, moreover, however, at least, in general, no doubt, by the bye, by the way, then, too, of course, in fine, namely, above all, therefore.

+Direction.+—*Write short sentences in which these words shall modify same particular word or phrase so closely as not to be set off by the comma*:—

Indeed, surely, too, then, now, further, why, again, still.

+Exercises on the Composition of the Sentence and the Paragraph.+

(SEE PAGES 160-162.)

TO THE TEACHER.—See suggestions to the teacher, pages 30, 150.

* * * * *

LESSON 46.

SENTENCES CLASSIFIED WITH RESPECT TO MEANING.

+Introductory Hints+.—In the previous Lessons we have considered the sentence with respect to the words and phrases composing it. Let us now look at it as a whole.

The mountains lift up their heads. This sentence is used simply to affirm, or to declare a fact, and is called a +Declarative Sentence.+

Do the mountains lift up their heads? This sentence expresses a question, and is called an +Interrogative Sentence.+

Lift up your heads. This sentence expresses a command, and is called an +Imperative Sentence+. Such expressions as *You must go, You shall go* are equivalent to imperative sentences, though they have not the imperative form.

How the mountains lift up their heads! In this sentence the thought is expressed with strong emotion. It is called an +Exclamatory Sentence+. *How* and *what* usually introduce such sentences; but a declarative, an interrogative, or an imperative sentence may become exclamatory when the speaker uses it mainly to give vent to his feelings; as, *It is impossible! How can I endure it! Talk of hypocrisy after this!*

+DEFINITION.—A *Declarative Sentence* is one that is used to affirm or to deny.+

+DEFINITION.—An *Interrogative Sentence* is one that expresses a question.+

+DEFINITION.—An *Imperative Sentence* is one that expresses a command or an entreaty.+

+DEFINITION.—An *Exclamatory Sentence* is one that expresses sudden thought or strong feeling.+ [Footnote: For punctuation, see page 42.]

+INTERROGATION POINT RULE. Every direct interrogative sentence should be followed by an interrogation point.+

+Remark.+—When an interrogative sentence is made a part of another sentence, it may be direct; as, He asked, "*What is the trouble?*" or indirect; as, He asked *what the trouble was.* (See Lesson 74.)

Analysis.

+Direction.+—*Before analyzing these sentences, classify them, and justify the terminal marks of punctuation:*—

1. There are no accidents in the providence of God. 2. Why does the very murderer, his victim sleeping before him, and his glaring eye taking the measure of the blow, strike wide of the mortal part? 3. Suffer not yourselves to be betrayed with a kiss.

(The subject is *you* understood.)

4. How wonderful is the advent of spring! 5. Oh! a dainty plant is the ivy green! 6. Six days shalt thou labor and do all thy work. 7. Alexander the Great died at Babylon in the thirty-third year of his age. 8. How sickness enlarges the dimensions of a man's self to himself! 9. Thou shalt not take the name of the Lord thy God in vain. 10. Lend me your ears. 11. What brilliant rings the planet Saturn has! 12. What power shall blanch the sullied snow of character? 13. The laws of nature are the thoughts of God. 14. How beautiful was the snow, falling all day long, all night long, on the roofs of the living, on the graves of the dead! 15. Who, in the darkest days of our Revolution, carried your flag into the very chops of the British Channel, bearded the lion in his den, and woke the echoes of old Albion's hills by the thunders of his cannon and the shouts of his triumph?

* * * * *

LESSON 47.

MISCELLANEOUS EXERCISES IN REVIEW

Analysis.

1. Poetry is only the eloquence and enthusiasm of religion.—*Wordsworth*.
2. Refusing to bare his head to any earthly potentate, Richelieu would permit no eminent author to stand bareheaded in his presence. —*Stephen*.
3. The Queen of England is simply a piece of historic heraldry; a flag, floating grandly over a Liberal ministry yesterday, over a Tory ministry to-day.—*Conway*.
4. The vulgar intellectual palate hankers after the titillation of foaming phrase.—*Lowell*.
5. Two mighty vortices, Pericles and Alexander the Great, drew into strong eddies about themselves all the glory and the pomp of Greek literature, Greek eloquence, Greek wisdom, Greek art.—*De Quincey*.
6. Reason's whole pleasure, all the joys of sense, lie in three words— health, peace, and competence.—*Pope*.
7. Extreme admiration puts out the critic's eye.—*Tyler*. [Footnote: Weighty thoughts tersely expressed, like (7), (8), and (10) in this Lesson, are called Epigrams. What quality do you think they impart to one's style?]
8. The setting of a great hope is like the setting of the sun.— *Longfellow*.
9. Things mean, the Thistle, the Leek, the Broom of the Plantagenets, become noble by association.—*F. W. Robertson*.
10. Prayer is the key of the morning and the bolt of the night.— *Beecher*.
11. In that calm Syrian afternoon, memory, a pensive Ruth, went gleaning the silent fields of childhood, and found the scattered grain still golden, and the morning sunlight fresh and fair.—*Curtis*. [Footnote:

In *Ruth* of this sentence, we have a type of the metaphor called +Personification+—a figure in which things are raised above their proper plane, taken up toward or to that of persons. Things take on dignity and importance as they rise in the scale of being.

Note, moreover, that in this instance of the figure we have an +Allusion+. All the interest that the Ruth of the Bible awakens in us this allusion gathers about so common a thing as memory.]

* * * * *

LESSON 48.

MISCELLANEOUS EXERCISES IN REVIEW.

Analysis.

1. By means of steam man realizes the fable of Aeolus's bag, and carries the two-and-thirty winds in the boiler of his boat.—*Emerson.*
2. The Angel of Life winds our brains up once for all, then closes the case, and gives the key into the hands of the Angel of Resurrection.—*Holmes.*
3. I called the New World into existence to redress the balance of the Old.—*Canning.*
4. The prominent nose of the New Englander is evidence of the constant linguistic exercise of that organ.—*Warner.*
5. Every Latin word has its function as noun or verb or adverb ticketed upon it.—*Earle.*
6. The Alps, piled in cold and still sublimity, are an image of despotism.—*Phillips.*
7. I want my husband to be submissive without looking so.—*Gail Hamilton.*

8. I love to lose myself in other men's minds.—*Lamb*.

9. Cheerfulness banishes all anxious care and discontent, soothes and composes the passions, and keeps the soul in a perpetual calm.—*Addison*.

10. To discover the true nature of comets has hitherto proved beyond the power of science.

+Explanation+.—*Beyond the power of science = impossible*, and is therefore an attribute complement. The preposition *beyond* shows the relation, in sense, of *power* to the subject phrase.

11. Authors must not, like Chinese soldiers, expect to win victories by turning somersets in the air.—*Longfellow*.

* * * * *

LESSON 49.

REVIEW OF PUNCTUATION.

+Direction+.—*Give the reasons, so far as you have been taught, for the marks of punctuation used in Lessons* 44, 46, 47, *and* 48.

* * * * *

LESSON 50.

REVIEW.

TO THE TEACHER.—See suggestions, Lesson 16.

+Direction+.—*Review from Lesson* 37 *to Lesson* 46, *inclusive*.

Give, in some such way as we have outlined in preceding Review Lessons, the substance of the "Introductory Hints;" repeat and illustrate definitions and rules; illustrate the different uses of the participle and the infinitive, and illustrate the Caution regarding the use of the participle; illustrate the different ways in which words and phrases may be grammatically independent, and the punctuation of these independent elements.

* * * * *

LESSON 51.

ARRANGEMENT—USUAL ORDER.

TO THE TEACHER.—If, from lack of time or from the necessity of conforming to a prescribed course of study, it is found desirable to abridge these Lessons on Arrangement and Contraction, the exercises to be written may be omitted, and the pupil may be required to illustrate the positions of the different parts, in both the Usual and the Transposed order, and then to read the examples given, making the required changes orally.

The eight following Lessons may thus be reduced to two or three.

Let us recall the +Usual Order+ of words and phrases in a simple declarative sentence.

The verb follows the subject, and the object complement follows the verb.

+Example+.—*Drake circumnavigated the globe.*

+Direction+.—*Observing this order, write three sentences each with an object complement.*

An adjective or a possessive modifier precedes its noun, and an explanatory modifier follows it.

+Examples+.—*Man's life is a brief span. Moses, the lawgiver,* came down from the Mount.

+Direction+.—*Observing this order, write four sentences, two with possessive modifiers and two with explanatory, each sentence containing an adjective.*

The attribute complement, whether noun or adjective, follows the verb, the objective complement follows the object complement, and the indirect object precedes the direct.

+Examples+.—Egypt *is the valley* of the Nile. Eastern life *is dreamy.* They made *Bonaparte consul.* They offered *Caesar a crown.*

+Direction+.—*Observing this order, write four sentences illustrating the positions of the noun and of the adjective when they perform these offices.*

If adjectives are of unequal rank, the one most closely modifying the noun stands nearest to it; if of the same rank, they stand in the order of their length—the shortest first.

+Examples+.—*Two honest young* men enlisted. Cassino has a *lean* and *hungry* look. A rock, *huge* and *precipitous,* stood in our path.

+Direction+.—*Observing this order, write three sentences illustrating the relative position of adjectives before and after the noun.*

An adverb precedes the adjective, the adverb, or the phrase which it modifies; precedes or follows (more frequently follows) the simple verb or the verb with its complement; and follows one or more words of the verb if the verb is compound.

+Examples+.—The light *far in the distance* is *so very* bright. I *soon* found him. I hurt him *badly*. He *had often been* there.

+Direction+.—*Observing this order, write sentences illustrating these several positions of the adverb.*

Phrases follow the words they modify; if a word has two or more phrases, those most closely modifying it stand nearest to it.

+Examples+.—*Facts once established* are facts forever. He *sailed for Liverpool on Monday*.

+Direction+.—*Observing this order, write sentences illustrating the positions of participle and prepositional phrases.*

* * * * *

LESSON 52.

ARRANGEMENT—TRANSPOSED ORDER.

+Introductory Hints+.—The usual order of words, spoken of in the preceding Lesson, is not the only order admissible in an English sentence; on the contrary, great freedom in the placing of words and phrases is sometimes allowable. Let the relation of the words be kept obvious and, consequently, the thought clear, and in poetry, in impassioned oratory, in excited speech of any kind, one may deviate widely from this order.

A writer's meaning is never distributed evenly among his words; more of it lies in some words than in others. Under the influence of strong feeling, one may move words out of their accustomed place, and, by thus attracting attention to them, give them additional importance to the reader or hearer.

When any word or phrase in the predicate stands out of its usual place, appearing either at the front of the sentence or at the end, we have what we may call the +Transposed Order+. *I dare not venture to go down into the cabin—Venture to go down into the cabin I dare not. You shall die—Die you shall. Their names will forever live on the lips of the people—Their names will, on the lips of the people, forever live.*

When the word or phrase moved to the front carries the verb, or the principal word of it, before the subject, we have the extreme example of the transposed order; as, *A yeoman had he. Strange is the magic of a turban.* The whole of a verb is not placed at the beginning of a declarative sentence except in poetry; as, *Flashed all their sabers bare.*

TO THE TEACHER.——Where, in our directions in these Lessons on Arrangement and Contraction, we say *change, transpose,* or *restore,* the pupils need not write the sentences. They should study them and be able to read them. Require them to show what the sentence has lost or gained in the change.

+Direction+.—*Change these sentences from the usual to the transposed order by moving words or phrases to the front, and explain the effect:*—

1. He could not avoid it. 2. They were pretty lads. 3. The great Queen died in the year 1603. 4. He would not escape. 5. I must go. 6. She seemed young and sad. 7. He cried, "My son, my son!" 8. He ended his tale here. 9. The moon shone bright. 10. A frozen continent lies beyond the sea. 11. He was a contentious man. 12. It was quoted so. 13. Monmouth had never been accused of cowardice.

+Direction+.—*Change these sentences from the transposed order to the usual, and explain the effect*:—

1. Him, the Almighty Power hurled headlong. 2. Volatile he was. 3. Victories, indeed, they were. 4. Of noble race the lady came. 5. Slowly and sadly we laid him down. 6. Once again we'll sleep secure. 7. This double office the participle performs. 8. That gale I well remember. 9. Churlish he often seemed. 10. One strong thing I find here below. 11. Overhead I heard a murmur. 12. To their will we must succumb. 13. Him they hanged. 14. Freely ye have received.

+Direction+.—*Write five sentences, each with one of the following nouns or adjectives as a complement; and five, each with one of the adverbs or phrases as predicate modifier; then transpose the ten with these same words moved to the front, and explain the effect*:—

Giant, character, happy, him, serene, often, in the market, long and deeply, then, under foot.

+Direction+.—*Transpose these sentences by placing the italicized words last, and note the effect*:—

1. The clouds lowering upon our house are *buried* in the deep bosom of the ocean. 2. Aeneas did *bear* from the flames of Troy upon his shoulder the old Anchises. 3. Such a heart *beats* in the breast of my people. 4. The great fire *roared* up the deep and wide chimney.

+Direction+.—*Change these to the usual order*:—

1. No woman was ever in this wild humor wooed and won. 2. Let a shroud, stripped from some privileged corpse, be, for its proper price, displayed. 3. An old clock, early one summer's morning, before the stirring

of the family, suddenly stopped. 4. Treasures of gold and of silver are, in the deep bosom of the earth, concealed. 5. Ease and grace in writing are, of all the acquisitions made in school, the most difficult and valuable.

+Direction+.—*Write three sentences, each with the following noun or adjective or phrase in its usual place in the predicate, and then transpose, placing these words wherever they can properly go:—*

Mountains, glad, by and by.

* * * * *

LESSON 53.

ARRANGEMENT—TRANSPOSED ORDER.

+Direction+.—*Restore these sentences to their usual order by moving the object complement and the verb to their customary places, and tell what is lost by the change:—*

1. Thorns and thistles shall the earth bring forth. 2. "Exactly so," replied the pendulum. 3. Me restored he to mine office. 4. A changed France have we. 5. These evils hath sin wrought.

+Direction+.—*Transpose these sentences by moving the object complement and the verb, and tell what is gained by the change:—*

1. The dial-plate exclaimed, "Lazy wire!" 2. The maiden has such charms. 3. The English character has faults and plenty of them. 4. I will make one effort more to save you. 5. The king does possess great power. 6. You have learned much in this short journey.

If the interrogative word is subject or a modifier of it, the order is usual.

+Examples+.—*Who* came last evening? *What star* shines brightest?

+Direction+.—*Write five interrogative sentences, using the first word below as a subject; the second as a subject and then as a modifier of the subject; the third as a subject and then as a modifier of the subject:—*

Who, which, what.

If the interrogative word is object complement or attribute complement or a modifier of either, the order is transposed.

+Examples+.—*Whom* did you see? *What* are personal consequences? *Which course* will you choose?

+Direction+.—*Write an interrogative sentence with the first word below as object complement, and another with the second word as attribute complement. Write four with the third and the fourth as complements, and four with the third and the fourth as modifiers of the complement:—*

Whom, who, which, what.

If the interrogative word is an adverb, the order is transposed.

+Examples+.—*Why* is the forum crowded? *Where* are the flowers, the fair young flowers?

+Direction+.—*Write five interrogative sentences, using these adverbs:—*

How, when, where, whither, why.

If there is no interrogative word, the subject stands after the verb when this is simple; after the first word of it when it is compound.

+Examples+.—*Have you* your lesson? *Has the gentleman* finished?

+Direction+.—*Write six interrogative sentences, using these words*:—

Is, has, can learn, might have gone, could have been found, must see.

+Direction+.—*Change the sentences you have written in this Lesson into declarative sentences.*

* * * * *

LESSON 56.

ARRANGEMENT—IMPERATIVE AND EXCLAMATORY SENTENCES.

The subject is usually omitted in the imperative sentence; but, when it is expressed, the sentence is in the transposed order.

+Examples+.—*Praise ye* the Lord. *Give* (*thou*) me three grains of corn.

+Direction+.—*Using these verbs, write ten sentences, in five of which the subject shall be omitted; and in five, expressed*:—

Remember, listen, lend, love, live, choose, use, obey, strive, devote.

Although any sentence may without change of order become exclamatory (Lesson 46), yet exclamatory sentences ordinarily begin with *how* or *what*, and are usually in the transposed order.

+Examples+.—*How quietly* the child sleeps! *How excellent* is thy loving-kindness! *What visions* have I seen! *What a life* his was!

+Direction+.—*Write six exclamatory sentences with the word* how *modifying (1) an adjective, (2) a verb, and (3) an adverb—in three sentences let the verb follow, and in three precede, the subject. Write four sentences with the word* what *modifying (1) an object complement and (2) an attribute complement—in two sentences let the verb follow, and in two precede, the subject.*

* * * * *

LESSON 57.

CONTRACTION OF SENTENCES.

+Direction+.—*Contract these sentences by omitting the repeated modifiers and prepositions, and all the conjunctions except the last:*—

1. Webster was a great lawyer, a great statesman, a great debater, and a great writer. 2. By their valor, by their policy, and by their matrimonial alliances, they became powerful. 3. Samuel Adams's habits were simple and frugal and unostentatious. 4. Flowers are so fragile, so delicate, and so ornamental! 5. They are truly prosperous and truly happy. 6. The means used were persuasions and petitions and remonstrances and resolutions and defiance. 7. Carthage was the mistress of oceans, of kingdoms, and of nations.

+Direction+.—*Expand these by repeating the adjective, the adverb, the preposition, and the conjunction:*—

1. He was a good son, father, brother, friend. 2. The tourist traveled in Spain, Greece, Egypt, and Palestine. 3. Bayard was very brave, truthful, and chivalrous. 4. Honor, revenge, shame, and contempt inflamed his heart.

+Direction+.—*Write six sentences, each with one of these words used four times; and then contract them as above, and note the effect of the repetition and of the omission:—*

Poor, how, with, through, or, and.

+Direction+.—*Expand these sentences by supplying subjects:—*

1. Give us this day our daily bread. 2. Why dost stare so? 3. Thank you, sir. 4. Hear me for my cause. 5. Where hast been these six months? 6. Bless me! 7. Save us.

+Direction+.—*Expand these by supplying the verb or some part of it:—*

1. Nobody there. 2. Death to the tyrant. 3. All aboard! 4. All hands to the pumps! 5. What to me fame? 6. Short, indeed, his career. 7. When Adam thus to Eve. 8. I must after him. 9. Thou shalt back to France. 10. Whose footsteps these?

+Direction+.—*Expand these by supplying both subject and verb, and note the loss in vivacity:—*

1. Upon them with the lance. 2. At your service, sir. 3. Why so unkind? 4. Forward, the light brigade! 5. Half-past nine. 6. Off with you. 7. My kingdom for a horse! 8. Hence, you idle creatures! 9. Coffee for two. 10. Shine, sir? 11. Back to thy punishment, false fugitive. 12. On with the dance. 13. Strange, strange! 14. Once more unto the breach. 15. Away, away! 16. Impossible!

+Direction+.—*Contract these by omitting the subject or the verb:—*

1. Art thou gone? 2. Will you take your chance? 3. His career was ably run. 4. Are you a captain? 5. May long life be to the republic. 6. How great

is the mystery! 7. Canst thou wonder? 8. May a prosperous voyage be to you. 9. Are you here?

+Direction+.—*Contract these by omitting both subject and verb, and note the gain in force and animation:—*

1. I offer a world for sale. 2. Now, then, go you to breakfast. 3. Sit you down, soothless insulter. 4. I want a word with you, wife. 5. Those are my sentiments, madam. 6. Bring ye lights there. 7. It is true, sir. 8. We will drink a health to Preciosa. 9. I offer a penny for your thoughts. 10. Whither are you going so early?

+Direction+.—*Construct ten full sentences, using in each, one of these adverbs or phrases or nouns, and then contract the sentences by omitting both subject and verb:—*

Why, hence, to arms, silence, out, to your tents, peaches, room, for the guns, water.

* * * * *

LESSON 58.

REVIEW.

TO THE TEACHER.—See suggestions, Lesson 16.

+Direction+.—*Review from Lesson 51 to Lesson 57, inclusive.*

Illustrate the different positions—Usual and Transposed—that the words and phrases of a declarative sentence may take; illustrate the different positions of the parts of an interrogative, of an imperative, and of an exclamatory sentence; illustrate the different ways of contracting sentences.

Exercises on the Composition of the Sentence and the Paragraph.

(SEE PAGES 162-165.)

TO THE TEACHER.—See notes to the teacher, pages 30, 150.

* * * * *

LESSON 59.

COMPLEX SENTENCE—ADJECTIVE CLAUSE.

+Introductory Hints+.—The sentences given for analysis in the preceding Lessons contain each but one subject and one predicate. They are called +Simple Sentences+.

A discreet youth makes friends. In Lesson 17 you learned that you could expand the adjective *discreet* into a phrase, and say, A youth of discretion makes friends. You are now to learn that you can expand it into an expression that asserts, and say, A youth *that is discreet* makes friends. This part of the sentence and the other part, *A youth makes friends*, containing each a subject and a predicate, we call +Clauses+.

The adjective clause *that is discreet*, performing the office of a single word, we call a +Dependent Clause+; *A youth makes friends*, not performing such office, we call an +Independent Clause+.

The whole sentence, composed of an independent and a dependent clause, we call a +Complex Sentence+.

A dependent clause that does the work of an adjective is called an +Adjective Clause+.

Analysis.

1. They that touch pitch will be defiled.

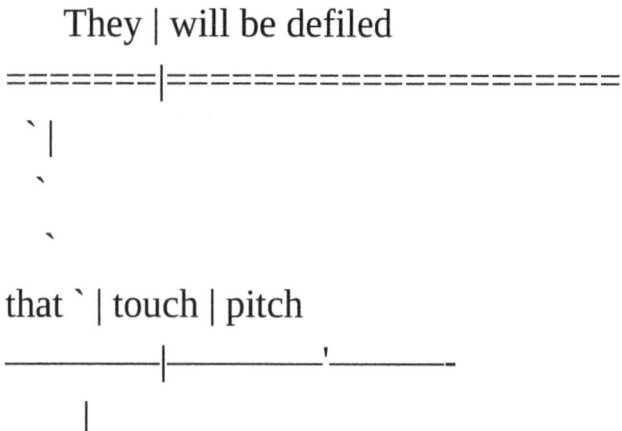

+Explanation+.—The relative importance of the two clauses is shown by their position, by their connection, and by the difference in the shading of the lines. The pronoun *that* is written on the subject line of the dependent clause. *That* performs the office of a conjunction also. This office is shown by the dotted line. As modifiers are joined by slanting lines to the words they modify, you learn from this diagram that *that touch pitch* is a modifier of *they*.

+Oral Analysis+.—This is a complex sentence because it consists of an independent clause and a dependent clause. *They will be defiled* is the independent clause, and *that touch pitch* is the dependent. *That touch pitch* is a modifier of *they* because it limits the meaning of *they*; the dependent clause is connected by its subject *that* to *they*.

TO THE TEACHER.—Illustrate the connecting force of *who, which*, and *that* by substituting for them the words for which they stand, and noting the loss of connection.

2. The lever which moves the world of mind is the printing-press. 3. Wine makes the face of him who drinks it to excess blush for his habits.

+Explanation+.—The adjective clause does not always modify the subject.

4. Photography is the art which enables commonplace mediocrity to look like
genius.
5. In 1685 Louis XIV. signed the ordinance that revoked the Edict of
Nantes.
6. The thirteen colonies were welded together by the measures which Samuel
Adams framed.

+Explanation+.—The pronoun connecting an adjective clause is not always a subject.

7. The guilt of the slave-trade, [Footnote: See Lesson 61, foot-note.] which sprang out of the traffic with Guinea, rests with John Hawkins. 8. I found the place to which you referred.

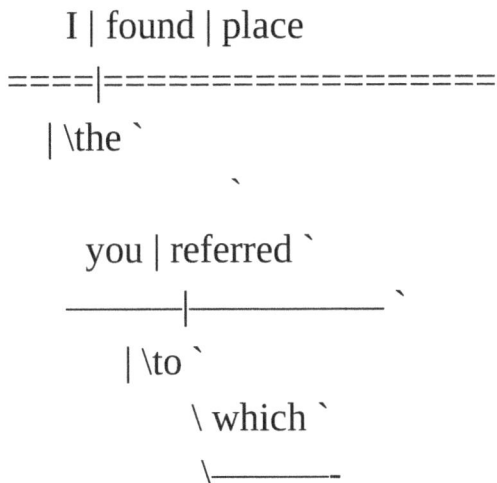

```
   I | found | place
====|=================
   | \the `
             `
    you | referred `
    ———|———— `
      | \to `
         \ which `
            \———-
```

9. The spirit in which we act is the highest matter. 10. It was the same book that I referred to.

+Explanation+.—The phrase *to that* modifies *referred*. *That* connects the adjective clause. When the pronoun *that* connects an adjective clause, the preposition never precedes. The diagram is similar to that of (8).

11. She that I spoke to was blind. 12. Grouchy did not arrive at the time that Napoleon most needed him.

+Explanation+.—A preposition is wanting. *That* = *in which*. (Can you find a word that would here sound better than *that*?)

13. Attention is the stuff that memory is made of. 14. It is to you that I speak.

+Explanation+.—Here the preposition, which usually would stand last in the sentence, is found before the complement of the independent clause. In analysis restore the preposition to its usual place—It is you that I speak *to*. *That I speak to* modifies the subject.

15. It was from me that he received the information.

(*Me* must be changed to *I* when *from* is restored to its usual position.)

16. Islands are the tops of mountains whose base is in the bed of the ocean.

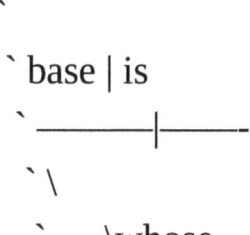

+Explanation+.—The connecting pronoun is here a possessive modifier of *base*.

17. Unhappy is the man whose mother does not make all mothers interesting.

* * * * *

LESSON 60.

ADJECTIVE CLAUSES—CONTINUED.

Analysis.

1. Trillions of waves of ether enter the eye and hit the retina in the time you take to breathe.

+Explanation+.—The connecting pronoun *that* [Footnote: When *whom*, *which*, and *that* would, if used, be object complements, they are often omitted. Macaulay is the only writer we have found who seldom or never omits them.] is omitted.

2. The smith takes his name from his smoothing the metals he works on. 3. Socrates was one of the greatest sages the world ever saw. 4. Whom the Lord loveth he chasteneth.

+Explanation+.—The adjective clause modifies the omitted antecedent of *whom*. Supply *him*.

5. He did what was right.

```
   He | did | x
====|====================
   | `
```

```
        `
   what ` | was \ right
   ─────────|─────────
```

+Explanation+.—The adjective clause modifies the omitted word *thing*, or some word whose meaning is general or indefinite. [Footnote: Many grammarians prefer to treat *what was right* as a noun clause (see Lesson 71), the object of *did*. They would treat in the same way clauses introduced by *whoever, whatever, whichever*.

"*What* was originally an interrogative and introduced substantive clauses. Its use as a compound relative is an extension of its use as an indirect interrogative; it is confined to clauses which may be parsed as substantives, and before which no antecedent is needed, or permitted to be expressed. Its possessive *whose* has, however, attained the full construction of a relative."—*Prof. F. A. March.*]

6. What is false in this world below betrays itself in a love of show. 7. The swan achieved what the goose conceived. 8. What men he had were true.

The relative pronoun *what* here precedes its noun like an adjective. Analyze as if arranged thus: The men *what* (= *that* or *whom*) he had were true.

9. Whoever does a good deed is instantly ennobled.

+Explanation+.—The adjective clause modifies the omitted subject (*man* or *he*) of the independent clause.

10. I told him to bring whichever was the lightest. 11. Whatever crushes individuality is despotism. 12. A depot is a place where stores are

deposited.

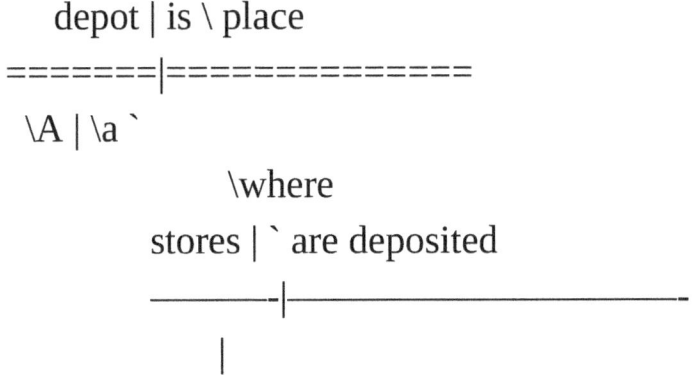

+Explanation+.—The line representing *where* is made up of two parts. The upper part represents *where* as a conjunction connecting the adjective clause to *place*, and the lower part represents it as an adverb modifying *are deposited*. As *where* performs these two offices, it may be called a *conjunctive adverb*. By changing *where* to the equivalent phrase *in which*, and using a diagram similar to (8), Lesson 59, the double nature of the conjunctive adverb will be seen.

13. He raised the maid from where she knelt. (Supply *the place* before *where*.) 14. Youth is the time when the seeds of character are sown. 15. Shylock would give the duke no reason why he followed a losing suit against Antonio. 16. Mark the majestic simplicity of those laws whereby the operations of the universe are conducted.

* * * * *

LESSON 61.

COMPOSITION—ADJECTIVE CLAUSE.

+COMMA—RULE.—The *Adjective Clause*, when not restrictive, is set off by the comma.+

+Explanation+.—I picked the apple *that was ripe*. I picked the apple, *which was ripe*. In the first sentence the adjective clause restricts or limits *apple*, telling which one was picked; in the second the adjective clause is added merely to describe the apple picked, the sentence being nearly equivalent to, I picked the apple, *and it* was ripe. This difference in meaning is shown by the punctuation.[Footnote: There are other constructions in which the relative is more nearly equivalent to *and he* or *and it*; as, I gave the letter to my friend, *who will return it to you.*

Those who prefer to let their classification be governed by the logical relation rather than by the grammatical construction call such a sentence compound, making the relative clause independent, or co-ordinate with its antecedent clause.

Such classification will often require very careful discrimination; as, for instance, between the preceding sentence and the following: I gave the letter to my friend, *who can be trusted*.

But we know of no author who, in every case, governs his classification of phrases and clauses strictly by their logical relations. Let us examine the following sentences:—

John, *who did not know the law*, is innocent. John is innocent; *he did not know the law*. John is innocent *because he did not know the law*.

No grammarian, we think, would class each of these three italicized clauses as an adverb clause of cause. Do they differ in logical force? The student should carefully note all those constructions in which the grammatical form and the logical force differ. (See pages 119, 121, 138, 139, 142, 143.)]

+Caution+.—The adjective clause should be placed as near as possible to the word it modifies.

+Direction+.—*Correct the following errors of position, and insert the comma when needed:—*

1. The Knights of the Round Table flourished in the reign of King Arthur who vied with their chief in chivalrous exploits. 2. Solomon was the son of David who built the Temple. 3. My brother caught the fish on a small hook baited with a worm which we had for breakfast. 4. I have no right to decide who am interested.

+Direction+.—*Construct five complex sentences, each containing an adjective clause equivalent to one of the following adjectives:—* Ambitious, respectful, quick-witted, talkative, lovable.

+Direction+.—*Change the following simple sentences to complex sentences by expanding the participle phrases into adjective clauses:—*

1. Those fighting custom with grammar are foolish. 2. The Constitution framed by our fathers is the sheet-anchor of our liberties. 3. I am thy father's spirit, doomed for a certain term to walk the night. 4. Some people, having lived abroad, undervalue the advantages of their native land. 5. A wife and children, threatened with widowhood and orphanage, have knelt at your feet on the very threshold of the Senate Chamber.

+Direction+.—*Change these simple sentences to complex sentences by expanding the infinitive phrases into adjective clauses:—*

1. I have many things to tell you. 2. There were none to deliver. 3. He had an ax to grind. 4. It was a sight to gladden the heart. 5. It was a din to fright a monster's ear.

+Direction+.—*Form complex sentences in which these pronouns and conjunctive adverbs shall be used to connect adjective clauses:*—

Who, which, that, what, whoever, and whatever.

When, where, and why.

+Direction+.—*Change "that which", in the following sentences to "what", and "what" to "that which"; "whoever" to "he who", and "whatever" to "anything" or "everything which"; "where" and "when" to "at", "on", or "in which"; "wherein" to "in which"; and "whereby" to "by which":*—

1. *That which* is seen is temporal. 2. *What* God hath joined together let not man put asunder. 3. *Whoever* lives a pious life blesses his race. 4. *Whatever* we do has an influence. 5. Scholars have grown old and blind, striving to put their hands on the very spot *where* brave men died. 6. The year *when* Chaucer was born is uncertain. 7. The play's the thing *wherein* I'll catch the conscience of the king. 8. You take my life in taking the means *whereby* I live.

+Direction+.—*Expand these possessive and explanatory modifiers into adjective clauses:*—

1. A man's heart deviseth *his* way. 2. *Reason's* whole pleasure, all the joys of sense, Lie in three words—*health, peace,* and *competence.*

* * * * *

LESSON 62.

+Direction+.—*Analyze the first nine sentences in the preceding Lesson, and write illustrative sentences as here directed:*—

Give an example of an adjective clause modifying a subject; one modifying a complement; one modifying the principal word of a phrase; one modifying some word omitted; one whose connective is a subject; one whose connective is a complement; one whose connective is the principal word of a phrase; one whose connective is a possessive modifier; one whose connective is omitted; one whose connective is an adverb.

* * * * *

LESSON 63.

COMPLEX SENTENCE—ADVERB CLAUSE.

+Introductory Hints+.—*He arrived late*. You have learned that you can expand the adverb *late* into a phrase, and say, He arrived *at midnight*. You are now to learn that you can expand it into a clause of +Time+, and say, He arrived *when the clock struck twelve*.

He stood where I am. The clause introduced by *where* expresses +Place+, and is equivalent to the adverb *here* or to the phrase *in this place*.

This exercise is as profitable as it is pleasant. The clause introduced by *as ... as* modifies *profitable*, telling the +Degree+ of the quality expressed by it.

A clause that does the work of an adverb is an +Adverb Clause+.

Analysis.

The +adverb clause+ may express +time+.

1. When pleasure calls, we listen.

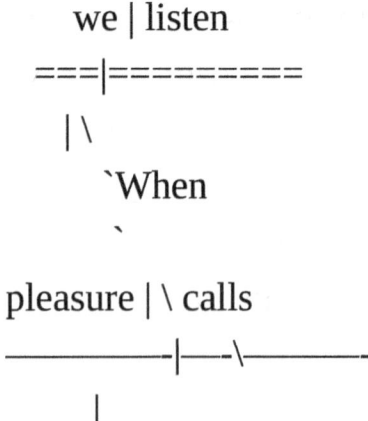

+Explanation+.—*When* modifies both *listen* and *calls,* denoting that the two acts take place at the same time. It also connects *pleasure calls,* as an adverb modifier, to *listen.* The offices of the conjunctive adverb *when* may be better understood by expanding it into two phrases thus: We listen *at the time at which* pleasure calls. *At the time* modifies *listen, at which* modifies *calls,* and *which* connects.

The line representing *when* is made up of three parts to picture these three offices. The part representing *when* as a modifier of *calls* is, for convenience, placed above its principal line instead of below it.

2. While Louis XIV. reigned, Europe was at war. 3. When my father and my mother forsake me, then ths Lord will take me up.

```
     Lord | will take | me
======|====================
\The | \up \
            ..\ then
              ` \
              `
                `When
     father \
                    -'\ \
```

```
   \my ' \ \
         ' \ \
         ' \ | \ forsake | me
         'and \———|————————————-
         ' / |
         ' /
   mother ' /
   ——————————'/
   \my
```

+Explanation+.—By changing *then* into *at the time*, and *when* into *at which*, the offices of these two words will be clearly seen. For explanation of the line representing *when*, see Lesson 14 and (1) above.

4. Cato, before he durst give himself the fatal stroke, spent the night in reading Plato's "Immortality." [Footnote: Some prefer, in constructions like this, to treat *before, ere, after, till, until,* and *since* as prepositions followed by noun clauses.]

5. Many a year is in its grave since I crossed this restless wave. [Footnote: See (11), Lesson 38, and foot-note.]

+Explanation+.—*Many* here modifies *year,* or, rather, *year* as modified by *a*.

6. Blucher arrived on the field of Waterloo just as Wellington was meeting the last onslaught of Napoleon.

```
   Blucher | arrived
==========|============
        | \
```

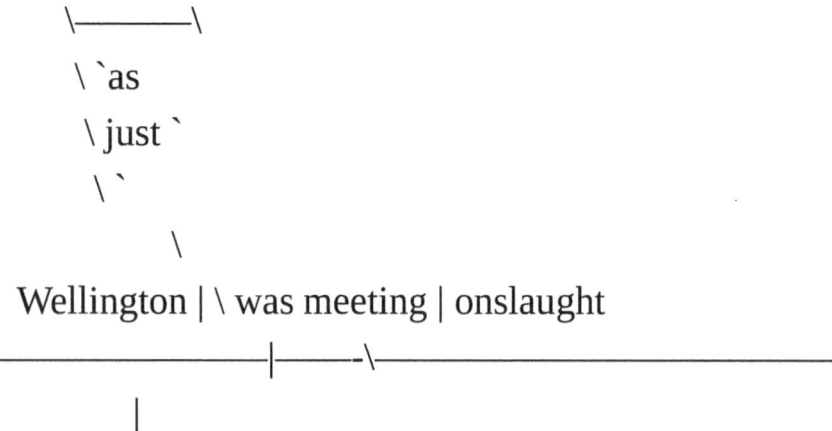

+Explanation+.—*Just* may be treated as a modifier of the dependent clause. A closer analysis, however would make it a modifier of *as*. *Just as=just at the time at which*. *Just* here modifies *at the time*. *At the time* is represented in the diagram by the first element of the *as* line.

The +adverb clause+ may express +place+.

7. Where the snow falls, there is freedom. 8. Pope skimmed the cream of good sense and expression wherever he could find it. 9. The wind bloweth where it listeth.

The +adverb clause+ may express +degree+.

10. Washington was as good as he was great.

+Explanation+.—The adverb clause *as he was great* modifies the first *as*, which is an adverb modifying *good*. The first *as*, modified by the adverb clause, answers the question, Good to what extent or degree? The second *as* modifies *great* and performs the office of a conjunction, and is therefore a conjunctive adverb. Transposing, and expanding *as … as* into two phrases, we have, Washington was good *in the degree in which* he was great. See diagram of (3) and of (20).

11. The wiser he grew, the humbler he became. [Footnote: *The*, here, is not the ordinary adjective *the*. It is the Anglo-Saxon demonstrative pronoun used in an instrumental sense. It is here an adverb. The first *the* = *by how much*, and modifies *wiser*; the second *the* = *by so much*, and modifies *humbler*.]

+Explanation+.—The words *the ... the* are similar in office to *as ... as*— He became humbler *in that degree in which* he became wiser.

12. Gold is heavier than iron.

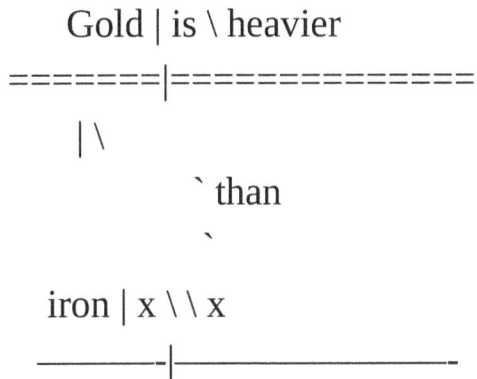

+Explanation+.—*Heavier* = *heavy beyond the degree*, and *than* = *in which*. The sentence = *Gold is heavy beyond the degree in which iron is heavy*. *Is* and *heavy* are omitted. Frequently words are omitted after *than* and *as*. *Than* modifies *heavy* (understood) and connects the clause expressing degree to *heavier*, and is therefore a conjunctive adverb.

13. To be right is better than to be president.

+Explanation+.—To be right is better (good in a greater degree) than to be president (would be good).

14. It was so cold that the mercury froze. [Footnote: In this sentence, also in (15) and (17), the dependent clause is sometimes termed a clause of

Result or Consequence. Clauses of Result express different logical relations, and cannot always be classed under Degree.]

+Explanation+.—The degree of the cold is here shown by the effect it produced. The adverb *so*, modified by the adverb clause *that the mercury froze*, answers the question, Cold to what degree? The sentence = It was cold *to that degree in which* the mercury froze. *That*, as you see, modifies *froze* and connects the clauses; it is therefore a conjunctive adverb.

15. It was so cold as to freeze the mercury.

+Explanation+.—It was so cold as to freeze the mercury (would indicate or require).

16. Dying for a principle is a higher degree of virtue than scolding for it. 17. He called so loud that all the hollow deep of hell resounded. 18. To preach is easier than to practice. 19. One's breeding shows itself nowhere more than in his religion. [Footnote: For the use of *he* instead of the indefinite pronoun *one* repeated, see Lesson 124.] 20. The oftener I see it, the better I like it.

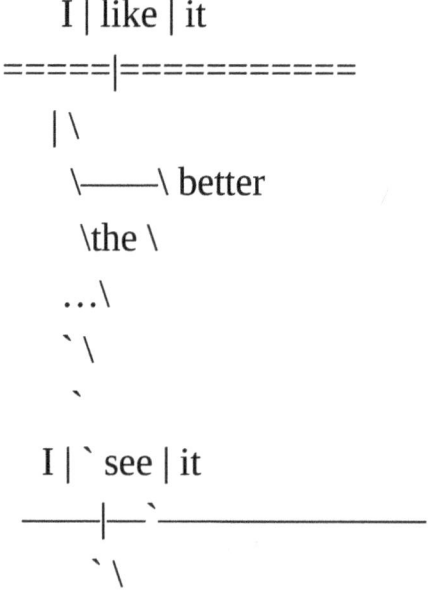

```
    `The \
     `.....\oftener
         \
```

* * * * *

LESSON 64.

ADVERB CLAUSE-CONTINUED.

+Introductory Hints+.—*He lived as the fool lives.* The adverb clause, introduced by *as*, is a clause of +Manner+, and is equivalent to the adverb *foolishly* or to the phrase *in a foolish manner*.

The ground is wet because it has rained. The adverb clause, introduced by *because*, assigns the +Real Cause+ of the ground's being wet.

It has rained, for the ground is wet. The adverb clause, introduced by *for*, does not assign the cause of the raining, but the cause of our believing that it has rained; it gives the +Evidence+ of what is asserted. [Footnote: Evidence should be carefully distinguished from Cause. Cause produces an effect; Evidence produces knowledge of an effect.

Clauses of Evidence are sometimes treated as independent.]

Analysis.

The +adverb clause+ may express +manner+.

1. He died as he lived.

+Explanation+.   He died *in the manner in which* he lived. For diagram, see (1), Lesson 63.

2. The upright man speaks as he thinks. 3. As the upright man thinks so he speaks.

(For diagram of *as … so,* see *when … then* (3), Lesson 63.)

4. As is the boy so will be the man. 5. The waves of conversation roll and shape our thoughts as the surf rolls and shapes the pebbles on the shore.

The +adverb clause+ may express +real cause+.

6. The ground is wet because it has rained.

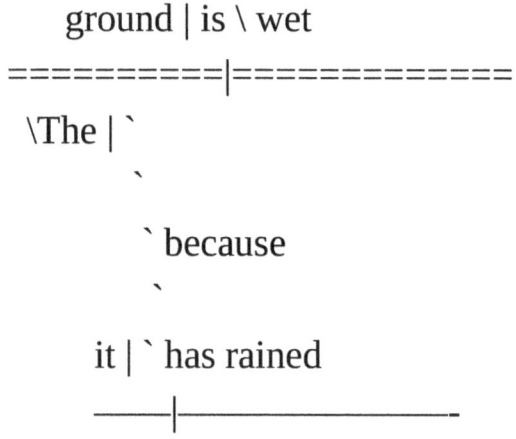

+Explanation+.—*Because,* being a mere conjunction, stands on a line wholly dotted.

7. Slang is always vulgar, as it is an affected way of talking. 8. We keep the pores of the skin open, for through them the blood throws off its impurities. 9. Since the breath contains poisonous carbonic acid, wise people ventilate their sleeping rooms. 10. Sea-bathing is the most healthful kind of washing, as it combines fresh air and vigorous exercise with its other benefits. 11. Wheat is the most valuable of grains because bread is made from its flour.

The +adverb clause+ may express +evidence+.

12. God was angry with the children of Israel, for he overthrew them in the wilderness. 13. Tobacco and the potato are American products, since Raleigh found them here. 14. It rained last night, because the ground is wet this morning. 15. We Americans must all be cuckoos, for we build our homes in the nests of other birds.

* * * * *

LESSON 65.

ADVERB CLAUSE-CONTINUED.

+Introductory Hints+.—*If it rains, the ground will be wet.* The adverb clause, introduced by *if*, assigns what, if it occurs, will be the cause of the ground's being wet, but, as here expressed, is only a +Condition+ ready to become a cause.

He takes exercise that he may get well. The adverb clause, introduced by *that*, assigns the cause or the motive or the +Purpose+ of his exercising.

The ground is dry, although it has rained. The adverb clause, introduced by *although*, expresses a +Concession+. It is conceded that a cause for the ground's not being dry exists; but, in spite of this opposing cause, it is asserted that the ground is dry.

All these dependent clauses of real cause, evidence, condition, purpose, and concession come, as you see, under the general head of +Cause+, although only the first kind assigns the cause proper.

Analysis.

The +adverb clause+ may express +condition+.

1. If the air is quickly compressed, enough heat is evolved to produce combustion.
2. Unless your thought packs easily and neatly in verse, always use prose. (*Unless* = *if not*.)
3. If ever you saw a crow with a king-bird after him, you have an image of a dull speaker and a lively listener.
4. Were it not for the warm waters of the Gulf Stream, the harbors and the rivers of Britain would be blocked up with ice for a great part of the year.

+Explanation+.—The relative position of the subject and the verb renders the *if* unnecessary. This omission of *if* is a common idiom.

5. Should the calls of hunger be neglected, the fat of the body is thrown into the grate to keep the furnace in play.

The +adverb clause+ may express +purpose+.

6. Language was given us that we might say pleasant things to each other.

+Explanation+.—*That*, introducing a clause of purpose, is a mere conjunction.

7. Spiders have many eyes in order that they may see in many directions at one time.

+Explanation+.—The phrases *in order that, so that* = *that*.

8. The ship-canal across the Isthmus of Suez was dug so that European vessels need not sail around the Cape of Good Hope to reach the Orient.
9. The air draws up vapors from the sea and the land, and retains them dissolved in itself or suspended in cisterns of clouds, that it may drop them as rain or dew upon the thirsty earth.

The +adverb clause+ may express +concession+.

10. Although the brain is only one-fortieth of the body, about one-sixth of the blood is sent to it.
11. Though the atmosphere presses on us with a load of fifteen pounds on every square inch of surface, still we do not feel its weight.
12. Though thou shouldst bray a fool in a mortar, yet will not his foolishness depart from him.
13. If the War of the Roses did not utterly destroy English freedom, it arrested its progress for a hundred years.

+Explanation+.—*If* here = *even if* = *though*.

14. Though many rivers flow into the Mediterranean, they are not sufficient to make up the loss caused by evaporation.

* * * * *

LESSON 66.

COMPOSITION-ADVERB CLAUSES.

+COMMA—RULE.—An *Adverb Clause* is set off by the comma unless it closely follows and restricts the word it modifies+.

+Explanation+.—I met him in Paris, *when I was last abroad.* I will not call him villain, *because it would be unparliamentary.* Paper was invented in China, *if the Chinese tell the truth.* In these sentences the adverb clauses are not restrictive, but are supplementary, and are added almost as afterthoughts.

Glass bends easily *when it is red-hot.* Leaves do not turn red *because the frost colors them.* It will break *if you touch it.* Here the adverb clauses are restrictive; each is very closely related in thought to the independent clause, and may almost be said to be the essential part of the sentence.

When the adverb clause precedes, it is set off.

+Direction+.—-*Tell why the adverb clauses are or are not set off in Lessons 63 and 64.*

+Direction+.—-_Write, after these independent clauses, adverb clauses of time, place, degree, etc. (for connectives, see Lesson *100*), and punctuate according to the Rule_:—

1. The leaves of the water-maple turn red—*time*. 2. Our eyes cannot bear the light—*time*. 3. Millions of soldiers sleep—*place*. 4. The Bunker Hill Monument stands—*place*. 5. Every spire of grass was so edged and tipped with dew—*degree*. 6. Vesuvius threw its lava so far—*degree*. 7. The tree is inclined—*manner*. 8. The lion springs upon his prey—*manner*. 9. Many persons died in the Black Hole of Calcutta—*cause*. 10. Dew does not form in a cloudy night—*cause*. 11. That thunderbolt fell a mile away—*evidence*. 12. We dream in our sleep—*evidence*. 13. Peter the Great worked in Holland in disguise—*purpose*. 14. We put salt into butter and upon meat—*purpose*. 15. Iron bends and molds easily—*condition*. 16. Apples would not fall to the ground—*condition*. 17. Europe conquered Napoleon at last—*concession*. 18. Punishment follows every violation of nature's laws—*concession*.

* * * * *

LESSON 67.

+COMPOSITION-ADVERB CLASSES+.

ARRANGEMENT.

The adverb clause may stand before the independent clause, between the parts of it, or after it.

+Direction+.—-*Think, if you can, of another adverb clause to follow each independent clause in the preceding Lesson, and by means of a caret (^) indicate where this adverb clause may properly stand in the sentence. Note its force in its several positions, and attend to the punctuation. Some of these adverb clauses can stand only at the end.*

* * * * *

LESSON 68.

COMPOSITION—ADVERB CLAUSES.

An adverb clause may be contracted into a participle or a participle phrase.

+Example+.—*When he saw me,* he stopped = *Seeing me,* he stopped.

+Direction+.—*Contract these complex sentences to simple ones:*—

1. Coral animals, when they die, form vast islands with their bodies. 2. The water will freeze, for it has cooled to 32 deg. 3. Truth, though she may be crushed to earth, will rise again. 4. Error, if he is wounded, writhes with pain, and dies among his worshipers. 5. Black clothes are too warm in summer, because they absorb heat.

An adverb clause may be contracted to an absolute phrase.

+Example+.—*When night came* on, we gave up the chase = *Night coming* on, we gave up the chase.

+Direction+.—*Contract these complex sentences to simple ones:*—

1. When oxygen and carbon unite in the minute blood-vessels, heat is produced. 2. It will rain to-morrow, for "Probabilities" predicts it. 3. Washington retreated from Long Island because his army was outnumbered. 4. If Chaucer is called the father of our later English poetry, Wycliffe should be called the father of our later English prose.

An adverb clause may be contracted to a prepositional phrase having for its principal word (1) a participle, (2) an infinitive, or (3) a noun.

+Direction+.—*Contract each of these adverb clauses to a prepositional phrase having a participle for its principal word:—*

+Model+.—They will call *before they leave* the city = They will call *before leaving* the city.

1. The Gulf Stream reaches Newfoundland before it crosses the Atlantic. 2. If we use household words, we shall be better understood. 3. He grew rich because he attended to his business. 4. Though they persecuted the Christians, they did not exterminate them.

+Direction+.—*Contract each of these adverb clauses to an infinitive phrase:—*

+Model+.—She stoops *that she may conquer* = She stoops *to conquer*.

1. The pine tree is so tall that it overlooks all its neighbors. 2. Philip II. built the Armada that he might conquer England. 3. He is foolish, because he leaves school so early in life. 4. What would I not give if I could see you happy! 5. We are pained when we hear God's name used irreverently.

+Direction+.—*Contract each of these adverb clauses to a prepositional phrase having a noun for its principal word:—*

+Model+.—He fought *that he might obtain glory* = He fought *for glory*.

1. Luther died where he was born. 2. A fish breathes, though it has no lungs. 3. The general marched as he was ordered. 4. Criminals are punished that society may be safe. 5. If you are free from vices, you may expect a happy old age.

An adverb clause may be contracted by simply omitting such words as may easily be supplied.

+Example+.—*When you are right*, go ahead = *When right*, go ahead.

+Direction+.—*Contract these adverb clauses*:—

1. Chevalier Bayard was killed while he was fighting for Francis I. 2. Error must yield, however strongly it may be defended.

+Explanation+.—*However* modifies *strongly*, and connects a concessive clause.

3. Much wealth is corpulence, if it is not disease. 4. No other English author has uttered so many pithy sayings as Shakespeare has uttered.

(Frequently, clauses introduced by *as* and *than* are contracted.)

5. The sun is many times larger than the earth is large.

(Sentences like this never appear in the full form.)

6. This is a prose era rather than it is a poetic era.

An adverb clause may sometimes be changed to an adjective clause or phrase.

+Example+.—This man is to be pitied, *because he has no friends* = This man, *who has no friends*, is to be pitied = This man, *having no friends*, is to be pitied = This man, *without friends*, is to be pitied.

+Direction+.—*Change each of the following adverb clauses first to an adjective clause and then to an adjective phrase:*—

1. A man is to be pitied if he does not care for music. 2. When a man lacks health, wealth, and friends, he lacks three good things.

* * * * *

LESSON 69.

ANALYSIS.

+Direction.+—_Tell the kind of adverb clause in each of the sentences in Lesson 68, and note the different positions in which these clauses stand.

Select two sentences containing time clauses; one, a place clause; two, degree; one, manner; two, real cause; two, evidence; two, purpose; two, condition; and two, concession, and analyze them_.

* * * * *

LESSON 70.

REVIEW.

+Direction.+—*Compose sentences illustrating the different kinds of adverb clauses named in Lessons 63, 64, 65, and explain fully the office of each. For connectives, see Lesson 100. Tell why the adverb clauses in Lesson 68 are or are not set off by the comma. Compose sentences illustrating the different ways of contracting adverb clauses.*

+Exercises on the Composition of the Sentence and the Paragraph.+

(SEE PAGES 165-168.)

TO THE TEACHER.—See suggestions to the teacher, pages 30, 150.

* * * * *

LESSON 71.

THE COMPLEX SENTENCE-NOUN CLAUSE.

+Introductory Hints.+—In Lessons 40 and 41 you learned that an infinitive phrase may perform many of the offices of a noun. You are now to learn that a clause may do the same.

Obedience is better than sacrifice = *To obey* is better than sacrifice = *That men should obey* is better than sacrifice. The dependent clause *that men should obey* is equivalent to a noun, and is the +Subject+ of *is*.

Many people believe that the beech tree is never struck by lightning. The dependent clause, introduced by *that*, is equivalent to a noun, and is the +Object Complement+ of *believe*.

The fact that mold, mildew, and yeast are plants is wonderful. The clause introduced by *that* is equivalent to a noun, and is +Explanatory+ of *fact*.

A peculiarity of English is, that it has so many borrowed words. The clause introduced by *that* is equivalent to a noun, and is an +Attribute Complement+ relating to *peculiarity*.

Your future depends very much on who your companions are. The clause *who your companions are* is equivalent to a noun, and is the +Principal Term+ of a +Phrase+ introduced by the preposition *on*.

A clause that does the work of a noun is a +Noun Clause+.

Analysis.

The +noun clause+ may be used as +subject+.

1. That the earth is round has been proved.

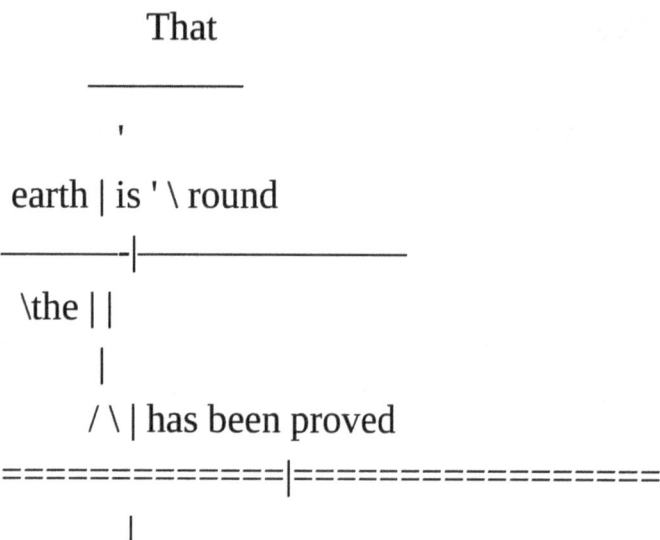

+Explanation+.—The clause *that the earth is round* is used like a noun as the subject of *has been proved*. The conjunction *that* [Footnote: "*That* was originally the neuter demonstrative pronoun, used to point to the fact stated in an independent sentence; as, It was good; he saw *that*. By an inversion of the order this became, He saw *that* (namely) it was good, and so passed into the form *He saw that it was good*, where *that* has been transferred to the accessory clause, and has become a mere sign of grammatical subordination."—*C. P. Mason.*] introduces the noun clause.

This is a peculiar kind of complex sentence. Strictly speaking, there is here no principal clause, for the whole sentence cannot be called a clause, *i.e.*, a part of a sentence. We may say that it is a complex sentence in which the whole sentence takes the place of a principal clause.

2. That the same word is used for the soul of man and for a glass of gin is singular. 3. "What have I done?" is asked by the knave and the thief. 4. Who was the discoverer of America is not yet fully determined by historians.

+Explanation+.—The subject clause is here an indirect question. See Lesson 74.

5. When letters were first used is not certainly known. 6. "Where is Abel, thy brother?" smote the ears of the guilty Cain. 7. When to quit business and enjoy their wealth is a problem never solved by some.

+Explanation+.—*When to quit business and enjoy their wealth* is an indirect question. *When to quit business = When they are to quit business*, or *When they ought to quit business*. Such constructions may be expanded into clauses, or they may be treated as phrases equivalent to clauses.

The +noun clause+ may be used as +object complement+.

8. Galileo taught that the earth moves.

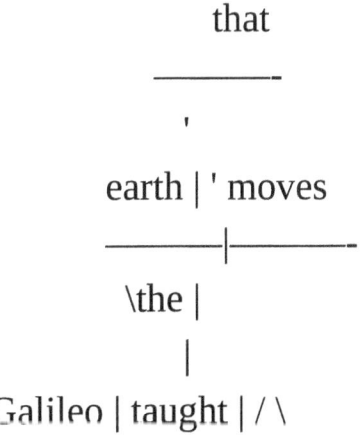

+Explanation+.—Here the clause introduced by *that* is used like a noun as the object complement of *taught*.

9. The Esquimau feels intuitively that bear's grease and blubber are the dishes for his table. 10. The world will not anxiously inquire who you are. 11. It will ask of you, "What can you do?" 12. The peacock struts about, saying, "What a fine tail I have!" 13. He does not know which to choose.

(See explanation of (7), above.)

14. No one can tell how or when or where he will die. 15. Philosophers are still debating whether the will has any control over the current of thought in our dreams.

* * * * *

LESSON 72.

NOUN CLAUSE—CONTINUED.

Analysis.

The +noun clause+ may be used as +attribute complement+.

1. A peculiarity of English is, that it has so many borrowed words. 2. Tweed's defiant question was, "What are you going to do about it?" 3. The question ever asked and never answered is, "Where and how am I to exist in the Hereafter?" 4. Hamlet's exclamation was, "What a piece of work is man!" 5. The myth concerning Achilles is, that he was invulnerable in every part except the heel.

The +noun clause+ may be used as +explanatory modifier+.

6. It has been proved that the earth is round.

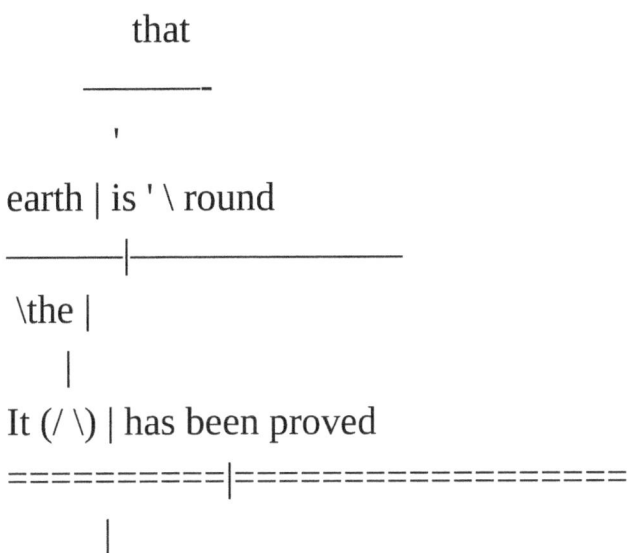

+Explanation+.—The grammatical subject *it* has no meaning till explained by the noun clause.

7. It is believed that sleep is caused by a diminution in the supply of blood to the brain. 8. The fact that mold, mildew, and yeast are plants is wonderful. 9. Napoleon turned his Simplon road aside in order that he might save a tree mentioned by Caesar.

+Explanation+.—Unless *in order that* is taken as a conjunction connecting an adverb clause of purpose (see (7), Lesson 65), the clause introduced by *that* is a noun clause explanatory of *order*. [Footnote: A similar explanation may be made of *on condition that, in case that*, introducing adverb clauses expressing condition.]

10. Shakespeare's metaphor, "Night's candles are burnt out," is one of the finest in literature.
11. The advice that St. Ambrose gave St. Augustine in regard to conformity

to local custom was in substance this: "When in Rome, do as the Romans do."

12. This we know, that our future depends on our present.

The +noun clause+ may be used as +principal term+ of a +prepositional phrase+.

13. Have birds any sense of why they sing?

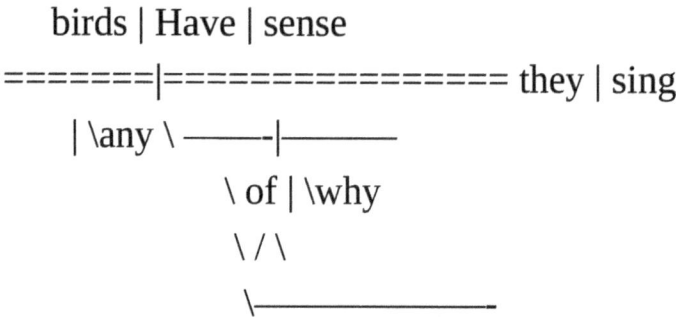

+Explanation+.—*Why they sing* is an indirect question, here used as the principal term of a prepositional phrase.

14. There has been some dispute about who wrote "Shakespeare's Plays." 15. We are not certain that an open sea surrounds the Pole.

+Explanation+.—By supposing *of* to stand before *that*, the noun clause may be treated as the principal term of a prepositional phrase modifying the adjective *certain*. By supplying *of the fact*, the noun clause will become explanatory.

16. We are all anxious that the future shall bring us success and triumph. 17. The Sandwich Islander is confident that the strength and valor of his slain enemy pass into himself.

* * * * *

LESSON 73.

COMPOSITION—NOUN CLAUSE.

+COMMA—RULE.—The *Noun Clause* used as attribute complement is generally set off by the comma.+

+Remarks+.—Present usage seems to favor the omission of the comma with the clause used as subject or as object complement, except where the comma would contribute to clearness.

The punctuation of the explanatory clause is like that of other explanatory modifiers. See Lesson 34. But the real subject made explanatory of *it* is seldom set off. See next Lesson for the punctuation of noun clauses that are questions or quotations.

+Direction+.—*Give the reasons for the use or the omission of the comma with the noun clauses in the preceding Lesson.*

By using *it* as a substitute for the subject clause, this clause may be placed last.

+Example+.—*That the story of William Tell is a myth is now believed* = *It is now believed that the story of William Tell is a myth.*

+Direction+.—*By the aid of the expletive it, transpose five subject clauses in Lesson 71.*

Often the clause used as object complement may be placed first.

+Direction+.—*Transpose such of the clauses used as object complements, in the preceding Lessons, as admit transposition. Punctuate*

If the direct quotation, whether a question or not, is formally introduced (see Lesson 147), it is preceded by the colon; as, Nathan's words to David were these: "*Thou art the man.*" He put the question thus: "*Can you do it?*"

+Direction+.—*Point out the direct and the indirect quotations and questions in the sentences of Lesson 71, tell why they do or do not begin with capital letters, and justify the use or the omission of the comma, the interrogation point, and the quotation marks.*

+Direction+.—*Rewrite these same sentences, changing the direct quotations and questions to indirect, and the indirect to direct.*

+Direction+.—*Write five sentences containing direct quotations, some of which shall be formally introduced, and some of which shall be questions occurring at the beginning or in the middle of the sentence. Change these to the indirect form, and look carefully to the punctuation and the capitalization.*

+Direction+.—*Write sentences illustrating the last paragraph of the Remarks under the Rule for Quotation Marks.*

* * * * *

LESSON 75.

ANALYSIS.

+Direction+.—*Analyze the sentences given for arrangement and contraction in Lesson 73.*

* * * * *

LESSON 76.

THE COMPOUND SENTENCE.

+Introductory Hints+.—*Cromwell made one revolution, and Monk made another.* The two clauses are independent of each other. The second clause, added by the conjunction *and* to the first, continues the line of thought begun by the first.

Man has his will, but woman has her way. Here the conjunction connects independent clauses whose thoughts stand in contrast with each other.

The Tudors were despotic, or history belies them. The independent clauses, connected by *or*, present thoughts between which you may choose, but either, accepted, excludes the other.

The ground is wet, therefore it has rained. Here the inferred fact, the raining, really stands to the other fact, the wetness of the ground, as cause to effect—the raining made the ground wet. *It has rained, hence the ground is wet.* Here the inferred fact, the wetness of the ground, really stands to the other fact, the raining, as effect to cause—the ground is made wet by the raining. But this the real, or logical relation between the facts in either sentence is expressed in a sentence of the compound form—an *and* may be placed before *therefore* and *hence*. Unless the connecting word expresses the dependence of one of the clauses, the grammarian regards them both as independent.

Temperance promotes health, intemperance destroys it. Here the independent clauses are joined to each other by their very position in the sentence—connected without any conjunction. This kind of connection is common.

Sentences made up of independent clauses we call +Compound Sentences.

+DEFINITION.—A *Clause* is a part of a sentence containing a subject and its predicate.+

+DEFINITION.—A *Dependent Clause* is one used as an adjective, an adverb, or a noun.+

+DEFINITION.—An *Independent Clause* is one not dependent on another clause.+

SENTENCES CLASSIFIED WITH RESPECT TO FORM.

+DEFINITION.—A *Simple Sentence* is a sentence that contains but one subject and one predicate, either or both of which may be compound.+

+DEFINITION.—A *Complex Sentence* is a sentence composed of an independent clause and one or more dependent clauses.+

+DEFINITION.—A *Compound Sentence* is a sentence composed of two or more independent clauses.+

Analysis.

+Independent Clauses+ in the +same line+ of thought.

1. Light has spread, and bayonets think.

```
  Light | has spread
=======|=============
   | '
     '
    ' and
   ........
      '
```

```
    bayonets | ' think
===========|==========
           |
```

+Explanation+.—The clauses are of equal rank, and so the lines on which they stand are shaded alike, and the line connecting them is not slanting. As one entire clause is connected with the other, the connecting line is drawn between the predicates merely for convenience.

+Oral Analysis+.—This is a compound sentence because it is made up of independent clauses.

2. Hamilton smote the rock of the national resources, and abundant streams
   of revenue gushed forth.
3. Some are born great, some achieve greatness, and some have greatness
   thrust upon them.

+Independent Clauses+ expressing thoughts in +contrast.+

4. The man dies, but his memory lives. 5. Put not your trust in money, but put your money in trust. 6. Ready writing makes not good writing, but good writing brings on ready writing.

+Independent Clauses+ expressing thoughts in +alternation+.

7. Be temperate in youth, or you will have to be abstinent in old age. 8. Places near the sea are not extremely cold in winter, nor are they extremely warm in summer.

(Here a choice is denied.)

9. Either Hamlet was mad, or he feigned madness admirably.

(See (16), Lesson 20.)

+Independent Clauses+ expressing thoughts one of which is an +inference+ from the other.

10. People in the streets are carrying umbrellas, hence it must be raining. 11. I have seen, therefore I believe.

```
  I | have seen
===|===========
  |'
   '
 I |' believe
===|='=========
  |\'
   \therefore
```

+Explanation+.—In such constructions *and* may be supplied, or the adverb may be regarded as the connective. The diagram illustrates *therefore* as connective.

+Independent Clauses+ joined in the sentence +without a conjunction+.

12. The camel is the ship of the ocean of sand; the reindeer is the camel of the desert of snow. 13. Of thy unspoken word thou art master; thy spoken word is master of thee. 14. The ship leaps, as it were, from billow to billow.

+Explanation+.—*As it were* is an independent clause used parenthetically. *As* simply introduces it.

15. Religion—who can doubt it?—is the noblest of themes for the exercise
   of intellect.
16. What grave (these are the words of Wellesley, speaking of the two
   Pitts) contains such a father and such a son!

* * * * *

LESSON 77.

COMPOSITION—COMPOUND SENTENCE.

+COMMA and SEMICOLON—RULE.—*Independent Clauses,* when short and closely connected, are separated by the+ +comma; but, when the clauses are slightly connected, or when they are themselves divided into parts by the comma, the semi-colon is used+.

+Remark+.—A parenthetical clause may be set oil by the comma or by the dash, or it may be inclosed within marks of parenthesis—the marks of parenthesis showing the least degree of connection in sense. See the last three sentences in the preceding Lesson.

+Examples+.—
1. We must conquer our passions, or our passions will conquer us.
2. The prodigal robs his heirs; the miser robs himself.
3. There is a fierce conflict between good and evil; but good is in the
   ascendant, and must triumph at last.

(The rule above is another example.)

+Direction+.—*Punctuate the following sentences, and give your reasons*:
—

1. The wind and the rain are over the clouds are divided in heaven over the
green hill flies the inconstant sun.
2. The epic poem recites the exploits of a hero tragedy represents a disastrous event comedy ridicules the vices and follies of mankind pastoral poetry describes rural life and elegy displays the tender emotions of the heart.
3. Wealth may seek us but wisdom must be sought.
4. The race is not to the swift nor the battle to the strong.
5. Occidental manhood springs from self-respect Oriental manhood finds its greatest satisfaction in self-abasement. [Footnote: In this sentence we have a figure of speech called +Antithesis+, in which things unlike in some particular are set over against each other. Each part shines with its own light and with the light reflected from the other part. Antithesis gives great force to the thought expressed by it. Sentences containing it furnish us our best examples of +Balanced Sentences+. You will find other antitheses in this Lesson and in the preceding.]
6. The more discussion the better if passion and personality be avoided and discussion even if stormy often winnows truth from error.

+Direction+.—*Assign reasons for the punctuation of the independent clauses in the preceding Lesson.*

+Direction+.—*Using the copulative and, the adversative but, and the alternative or or nor, form compound sentences out of the following simple sentences, and give the reasons for your choice of connectives:*—

Read not that you may find material for argument and conversation. The rain descended. Read that you may weigh and consider the thoughts of others. Can the Ethiopian change his skin? Righteousness exalteth a nation. The floods came. Great was the fall of it. Language is not the dress of thought. Can the leopard change his spots? The winds blew and beat upon that house. Sin is a reproach to any people. It is not simply its vehicle. It fell.

Compound sentences may be contracted by using but once the parts common to all the clauses, and compounding the remaining parts.

+Example+.—*Time* waits for no man, and *tide waits for no man* = *Time* and *tide wait for no man.*

+Direction+.—*Contract these compound sentences, attending carefully to the punctuation*:—

1. Lafayette fought for American independence, and Baron Steuben fought for
   American independence.
2. The sweet but fading graces of inspiring autumn open the mind to benevolence, and the sweet but fading graces of inspiring autumn dispose the mind for contemplation.
3. The spirit of the Almighty is within us, the spirit of the Almighty is around us, and the spirit of the Almighty is above us.

A compound sentence may be contracted by simply omitting from one clause such words as may readily be supplied from the other.

Example.—He is witty, *but he is vulgar* = He is witty *but vulgar*.

+Direction+.—*Contract these sentences*:—

1. Mirth should be the embroidery of conversation, but it should not be the web. 2. It is called so, but it is improperly called so. 3. Was Cabot the discoverer of America, or was he not the discoverer of America? 4. William the Silent has been likened to Washington, and he has justly been likened to

him. 5. It was his address that pleased me, and it was not his dress that pleased me.

A compound sentence may sometimes be changed to a complex sentence without materially changing the sense.

+Example+.—*Take care of the minutes,* and the hours will take care of themselves = *If you take care of the minutes,* the hours will take care of themselves. (Notice that the imperative form adds force.)

+Direction+.—*Change these compound sentences to complex sentences*:—

1. Resist the devil, and he will flee from you. 2. Govern your passions, or they will govern you. 3. I heard that you wished to see me, and I lost no time in coming. 4. He converses, and at the same time he plays a difficult piece of music. 5. He was faithful, and he was rewarded.

+Direction+.—*Change one of the independent clauses in each of these sentences to a dependent clause, and then change the dependent clause to a participle phrase*:—

+Model+.—The house was built upon a rock, *and therefore* it did not fall = The house did not fall, *because* it was built upon a rock = The house, *being built* upon a rock, did not fall.

1. He found that he could not escape, and so he surrendered. 2. Our friends heard of our coming, and they hastened to meet us.

+Direction+.—*Using and, but, and or as connectives, compose three compound sentences, each containing three independent clauses.*

* * * * *

LESSON 78.

COMPLEX AND COMPOUND CLAUSES.

+Introductory Hints+.—*Sun and moon and stars* obey. Peter the Great went *to Holland, to England,* and *to France. I came, I saw, I conquered.* Here we have co-ordinate words, co-ordinate phrases, and co-ordinate clauses, that is, words, phrases, and clauses of equal rank, or order.

Leaves fall *so very quietly.* They ate *of the fruit from the tree in the garden.* Regulus would have paused *if he had been the man that he was before captivity had unstrung his sinews.* Here just as the word modifier *quietly* is itself modified by *very*, and *very* by *so*; and just as *fruit*, the principal word in a modifying phrase, is modified by another phrase, and the principal word of that by another: so *man*, in the adverb clause which modifies *would have paused*, is itself modified by the adjective clause *that he was*, and *was* by the adverb clause *before captivity had unstrung his sinews*. These three dependent clauses in the complex clause modifier, like the three words and the three phrases in the complex word modifier and the complex phrase modifier, are not co-ordinate, or of equal rank.

Mary married Philip; but Elizabeth would not marry, although Parliament frequently urged it, and the peace of England demanded it. This is a compound sentence, composed of the simple clause which precedes *but* and the complex clause which follows it—the complex clause being composed of an independent clause and two dependent clauses, one co-ordinate with the other, and the two connected by *and*.

Analysis.

The +clauses+ of +complex+ and +compound+ sentences may themselves be +complex+ or +compound+.

```
              insects
         _____
      ` ` `
        ` ` `which | are admired
         ` ` `=====|=============
          ` ` | '
           ` ` ' x
            ` `
               …..
             ` ` '
              ` `which | are decorated
               ` ======|===============
                ` | '
                 ` 'and
                  `
                    ……..
                   ` '
                    ` which | soar '
                     `======|=======
                            |
         hour | had passed
    ========|=============
     \The |` '
             ` ' and
              `
                …….
               ` '
    opportunity | ` had escaped
    ============|==`============
        \the | ` \
                 ` '
                   ` '
                     ` '
```

```
                `while
              `
        he | ` tarried
       ——|——————-
          |
         that
        ————-
          ,
   earth | ' is \ round
   ========|======'========
          | '
      that ' and
       ————- ……
         ' '
     it | ' revolves '
     ===|='============'=
          |
He | proved | / \
====|=============
   |
```

+Explanation+.—The first diagram illustrates the analysis of the compound adjective clause in (3) below. Each adjective clause is connected to *insects* by *which*. *And* connects the co-ordinate clauses. The second diagram shows that the clause *while he tarried* modifies both predicates of the independent clauses. *While* modifies *had passed*, *had escaped*, and *tarried*, as illustrated by the short lines under the first two verbs and the line over *tarried*. The office of *while* as connective is shown by the dotted lines. The third diagram illustrates the analysis of a complex sentence containing a compound noun clause.

1. Sin has a great many tools, but a lie is a handle which fits them all.
2. Some one has said that the milkman's favorite song should be, "Shall we gather at the river?"
3. Some of the insects which are most admired, which are decorated with the most brilliant colors, and which soar on the most ethereal wings, have passed the greater portion of their lives in the bowels of the earth.
4. Still the wonder grew, that one small head could carry all he knew.
5. When a man becomes overheated by working, running, rowing, or making furious speeches, the six or seven millions of perspiration tubes pour out their fluid, and the whole body is bathed and cooled.
6. Milton said that he did not educate his daughters in the languages, because one tongue was enough for a woman. [Footnote: In *tongue*, as here used, we have a +Pun+—a witty expression in which a word agreeing in sound with another word, but differing in meaning from it, is used in place of that other.]
7. Glaciers, flowing down mountain gorges, obey the law of rivers; the upper surface flows faster than the lower, and the center faster than the adjacent sides.
8. Not to wear one's best things every day is a maxim of New England thrift, which is as little disputed as any verse in the catechism.
9. In Holland the stork is protected by law, because it eats the frogs and worms that would injure the dikes.
10. It is one of the most marvelous facts in the natural world that, though hydrogen is highly inflammable, and oxygen is a supporter of combustion, both, combined, form an element, water, which is destructive to fire.
11. In your war of 1812, when your arms on shore were covered by disaster,

when Winchester had been defeated, when the Army of the Northwest had surrendered, and when the gloom of despondency hung, like a cloud, over the land, who first relit the fires of national glory, and made the welkin ring with the shouts of victory? [Footnote: The *when* clauses in (11), as the *which* clauses in (3), are formed on the same plan, have their words in the same order. This principle of +Parallel Construction+, requiring like ideas to be expressed alike, holds also in phrases, as in (10) and (14), Lesson 28, and in (14) and (15), Lesson 46, and holds supremely with sentences in the paragraph, as is explained on page 168. Parallel construction contributes to the clearness, and consequently to the force, of expression.]

* * * * *

LESSON 79.

EXPANSION.

+Participles+ may be expanded into different kinds of +clauses+.

+Direction+.—*Expand the participles in these sentences into the clauses indicated*:—

1. Simon Peter, having a sword, drew it. (Adjective clause.) 2. Desiring to live long, no one would be old. (Concession.) 3. They went to the temple, suing for pardon. (Purpose.) 4. White garments, reflecting the rays of the sun, are cool in summer. (Cause.) 5. Loved by all, he must have a genial disposition. (Evidence.) 6. Writing carefully, you will learn to write well. (Condition.) 7. Sitting there, I heard the cry of "Fire!" (Time.) 8. She regrets

not having read it. (Noun clause.) 9. The icebergs floated down, cooling the air for miles around, (Independent clause.)

+Absolute phrases+ may be expanded into different kinds of +clauses+.

+Direction+.—*Expand these absolute phrases into the clauses indicated*:—

1. Troy being taken by the Greeks, Aeneas came into Italy. (Time.) 2. The bridges having been swept away, we returned. (Cause.) 3. A cause not preceding, no effect is produced. (Condition.) 4. All things else being destroyed, virtue could sustain itself. (Concession.) 5. There being no dew this morning, it must have been cloudy or windy last night. (Evidence.) 6. The infantry advanced, the cavalry remaining in the rear. (Independent clause.)

+Infinitive+ phrases may be expanded into different kinds of +clauses+.

+Direction+.—*Expand these infinitive phrases into the clauses indicated*:—

1. They have nothing to wear. (Adjective clause.) 2. The weather is so warm as to dissolve the snow. (Degree.) 3. Herod will seek the young child to destroy it. (Purpose.) 4. The adversative sentence faces, so to speak, half way about on *but*. (Condition.) 5. He is a fool to waste his time so. (Cause.) 6. I shall be happy to hear of your safe arrival. (Time.) 7. He does not know where to go. (Noun clause.)

+Direction+.—*Complete these elliptical expressions*:—

1. And so shall Regulus, though dead, fight as he never fought before. 2. Oh, that I might have one more day! 3. He is braver than wise. 4. What if he is poor? 5. He handles it as if it were glass. 6. I regard him more as a

historian than as a poet. 7. He is not an Englishman, but a Frenchman. 8. Much as he loved his wealth, he loved his children better. 9. I will go whether you go or not. 10. It happens with books as with mere acquaintances. 11. No examples, however awful, sink into the heart.

* * * * *

LESSON 80.

MISCELLANEOUS EXERCISES IN REVIEW.

Analysis.

1. Whenever the wandering demon of Drunkenness finds a ship adrift, he steps on board, takes the helm, and steers straight for the Maelstrom.—*Holmes*.
2. The energy which drives our locomotives and forces our steamships through the waves comes from the sun.—*Cooke*.
3. No scene is continually loved but one rich by joyful human labor, smooth in field, fair in garden, full in orchard.—*Ruskin*.
4. What is bolder than a miller's neck-cloth, which takes a thief by the throat every morning?—*German Proverb*.
5. The setting sun stretched his celestial rods of light across the level landscape, and smote the rivers and the brooks and the ponds, and they became as blood.—*Longfellow*.
6. Were the happiness of the next world as closely apprehended as the felicities of this, it were a martyrdom to live.—*Sir T. Browne*.
7. There is a good deal of oratory in me, but I don't do as well as I can, in any one place, out of respect to the memory of Patrick Henry.—*Nasby*.
8. Van Twiller's full-fed cheeks, which seemed to have taken toll of everything that went into his mouth, were curiously mottled and streaked

with dusky red, like a spitzenburg apple.—*Irving.*

9. The evil of silencing the expression of an opinion is, that it is robbing the human race.—*Mill.*
10. There is no getting along with Johnson; if his pistol misses fire, he knocks you down with the butt of it.—*Goldsmith.*
11. We think in words; and, when we lack fit words, we lack fit thoughts.—*White.*
12. To speak perfectly well one must feel that he has got to the bottom of his subject.—*Whately.*
13. Office confers no honor upon a man who is worthy of it, and it will disgrace every man who is not.—*Holland.*
14. The men whom men respect, the women whom women approve, are the men and
    women who bless their species.—*Parton.*

* * * * *

LESSON 81.

MISCELLANEOUS EXERCISES IN REVIEW.

Analysis.

1. A ruler who appoints any man to an office when there is in his dominions
    another man better qualified for it sins against God and against the
    state.—*Koran.*
2. We wondered whether the saltness of the Dead Sea was not Lot's wife in solution.—*Curtis.*
3. There is a class among us so conservative that they are afraid the roof will come down if you sweep off the cobwebs.—*Phillips.*
4. Kind hearts are more than coronets; and simple faith, than Norman

blood.—*Tennyson.*

5. All those things for which men plow, build, or sail obey virtue.—*Sallust.*

6. The sea licks your feet, its huge flanks purr very pleasantly for you; but it will crack your bones and eat you for all that.—*Holmes.*

7. Of all sad words of tongue or pen the saddest are these: "It might have been."—*Whittier.*

8. I fear three newspapers more than a hundred thousand bayonets.—*Napoleon.*

9. He that allows himself to be a worm must not complain if he is trodden on.—*Kant.*

10. It is better to write one word upon the rock than a thousand on the water or the sand.—*Gladstone.*

11. A breath of New England's air is better than a sup of Old England's ale.—*Higginson.*

12. We are as near to heaven by sea as by land.—*Sir H. Gilbert.*

13. No language that cannot suck up the feeding juices secreted for it in the rich mother-earth of common folk can bring forth a sound and lusty book.—*Lowell.*

14. Commend me to the preacher who has learned by experience what are human

    ills and what is human wrong.—*Boyd.*

15. He prayeth best who loveth best all things both [Footnote: See Lesson 20.] great and small; for the dear God, who loveth us, he made and loveth all.—*Coleridge.*

* * * * *

LESSON 82.

REVIEW.

Show that an adjective may be expanded into an equivalent phrase or clause. Give examples of adjective clauses connected by *who, whose, which, what, that, whichever, when, where, why,* and show that each connective performs also the office of a pronoun or that of an adverb. Give and illustrate fully the Rule for punctuating the adjective clause, and the Caution regarding the position of the adjective clause. Show that an adjective clause may be equivalent to an Infinitive phrase or a participle phrase.

Show that an adverb may be expanded into an equivalent phrase or clause. Illustrate the different kinds of adverb clauses, and explain the office of each and the fitness of the name. Give and explain fully the Rule for the punctuation of adverb clauses. Illustrate the different positions of adverb clauses. Illustrate the different ways of contracting adverb clauses.

* * * * *

LESSON 83.

REVIEW.

Illustrate five different offices of a noun clause. Explain the two different ways of treating clauses introduced by *in order that*, etc. Explain the office of the expletive *it*. Illustrate the different positions of a noun clause used as object complement. Show how the noun clause may be made prominent. Illustrate the different ways of contracting noun clauses. Give and illustrate fully the Rule for quotation marks. Illustrate and explain fully the distinction between direct and indirect quotations, and the distinction between direct and indirect questions introduced into a sentence. Tell all about their capitalization and punctuation.

* * * * *

LESSON 84.

REVIEW.

Illustrate and explain the distinction between a dependent and an independent clause. Illustrate and explain the different ways in which independent clauses connected by *and, but, or,* and *hence* are related in sense. Show how independent clauses may be joined in sense without a connecting word. Define a clause. Define the different kinds of clauses. Define the different classes of sentences with regard to form. Give the Rule for the punctuation of independent clauses, and illustrate fully. Illustrate the different ways of contracting independent clauses. Illustrate and explain the difference between compound and complex word modifiers; between compound and complex phrases; between compound and complex clauses. Give participle phrases, absolute phrases, and infinitive phrases, and expand them into different kinds of clauses. What three parts of speech may connect clauses?

GENERAL REVIEW.

TO THE TEACHER.—This scheme will be found very helpful in a general review. The pupils should be able to reproduce it except the Lesson numbers.

Scheme for the Sentence.

(*The numbers refer to Lessons.*)

+PARTS.+

+Subject.+
Noun or Pronoun (8).

Phrase (38, 40).
Clause (71).

   +Predicate.+
Verb (11).

   +Complements.+
+Object.+
  Noun or Pronoun (28).
  Phrase (38, 40).
  Clause (71).
+Attribute.+
  Adjective (29, 30).
  Participle (37).
  Noun or Pronoun (29, 30).
  Phrase (37, 40).
  Clause (72).
+Objective.+
  Adjective (31).
  Participle (37).
  Noun (or Pronoun) (31).
  Phrase (37, 41).

   +Modifiers.+
Adjectives (12).
Adverbs (14).
Participles (37).
Nouns and Pronouns (33, 35).
Phrases (17, 37, 38, 40, 41).
Clauses (59, 60, 63, 64, 65).

+Connectives.+
Conjunctions (20, 64, 65, 71, 76).
Pronouns (59, 60).
Adverbs (60, 63, 64).

+Independent Parts+ (44).

+Classes.+
+Meaning.+ Declarative, Interrogative, Imperative, Exclamatory (46).
+Form.+ Simple, Complex, Compound (76).

Additional Selections.

TO THE TEACHER.—We believe that you will find the preceding pages unusually full and rich in illustrative selections; but, should additional work be needed for reviews or for maturer classes, the following selections will afford profitable study. Let the pupils discuss the thought and the poetic form, as well as the logical construction of these passages. We do not advise putting them in diagram.

> Speak clearly, if you speak at all;
> Carve every word before you let it fall.—*Holmes.*

> The robin and the blue-bird, piping loud,
>   Filled all the blossoming orchards with their glee;
> The sparrows chirped as if they still were proud
>   Their race in Holy Writ should mentioned be;
> And hungry crows, assembled in a crowd,
>   Clamored their piteous prayer incessantly,
> Knowing who hears the ravens cry, and said,

"Give us, O Lord, this day, our daily bread!"
—*Longfellow*,

   Better to stem with heart and hand
   The roaring tide of life than lie,
Unmindful, on its flowery strand,
   Of God's occasions drifting by.
   Better with naked nerve to bear
   The needles of this goading air
Than, in the lap of sensual ease, forego
The godlike power to do, the godlike aim to know.
—*Whittier*.

   Then to side with Truth is noble when we share her wretched crust,
Ere her cause bring fame and profit, and 't is prosperous to be just;
Then it is the brave man chooses, while the coward stands aside,
Doubting in his abject spirit, till his Lord is crucified.—*Lowell*.

Exercises on the Composition of the Sentence and the Paragraph.

TO THE TEACHER.—These and similar "Exercises" are entirely outside of the regular lessons. They are offered to those teachers who may not, from lack of time or of material, find it convenient to prepare extra or miscellaneous work better suited to their own needs.

The questions appended to the following sentences are made easy of answer, but in continuing such exercises the teacher will, of course, so frame the questions as more and more to throw responsibility on the pupil.

It will be evident that this work aims not only to enforce instruction given before Lesson 17, but, by an easy and familiar examination of words and groups of words, to prepare the way for what is afterwards presented more formally and scientifically. ADAPTED FROM IRVING'S "SKETCH BOOK."

1. From this piazza the wondering Ichabod entered the hall. 2. This hall formed the center of the mansion and the place of usual residence. 3. Here, rows of resplendent pewter, ranged on a long dresser, dazzled his eyes. 4. In one corner stood a huge bag of wool ready to be spun. 5. In another corner stood a quantity of linsey-woolsey just from the loom. 6. Ears of Indian corn and strings of dried apples and peaches hung in gay festoons along the walls. 7. These were mingled with the gaud of red peppers. 8. A door left ajar gave him a peep into the best parlor. 9. In this parlor claw-footed chairs and dark mahogany tables shone like mirrors. 10. Andirons, with their accompanying shovel and tongs, glistened from their covert of asparagus tops. [Footnote: *Asparagus tops* were commonly used to ornament the old-fashioned fireplace in summer.] 11. Mock-oranges and conch-shells decorated the mantelpiece. 12. Strings of various-colored birds' eggs were suspended above it. 13. A corner-cupboard, knowingly left open, displayed immense treasures of old silver and well-mended china.

+The Uses of Words and Groups of Words+.—Find the two chief words in each of the first three sentences. As a part of the sentence what is each of these words called? To what class of words, or part of speech, does each belong? Notice that in the fourth and the fifth sentence the subject is put after the predicate. Change the order of words and read these sentences. Read in their regular order the two chief words of each. In the sixth sentence what word says, or asserts, something about both ears and strings? In the ninth sentence put *what* before the predicate *shone* and find two nouns that answer the question. In the eleventh sentence what two things does *decorated* tell something about? In the seventh sentence *these* stands for what two nouns, or names, found in the preceding sentence? Find the subject and the predicate of each sentence from the sixth to the thirteenth inclusive. To what class of words does each of these chief parts belong? Find in these sentences nouns that are not subjects. Find several compound nouns the parts of which are joined with the hyphen.

The and *wondering* in the first sentence go with what noun? The group of words *from this piazza* goes with what word? In the second sentence put *what* before, and then after, *formed,* and find the names that answer these questions. What does *of the mansion* go with? What does *of usual residence* describe? In the third sentence what word tells where the dazzling occurred? Find a group of three words telling what the rows were composed of. What group of words tells the position of the rows? In the fourth sentence what group of words shows where the bag stood? *Of wool ready to be spun* describes what? *A* and *huge* are attached to what?

TO THE TEACHER.—We have here suggested some of the devices by which pupils may be led to see the functions of words and phrases. We recommend that this work be varied and continued through the selection above and through others that may easily be made. Such exercises, together with the more formal and searching work of the regular lessons, will be found of incalculable value to the pupil. They will not only afford the best mental discipline but will aid greatly in getting thought and in expressing thought.

+The Force and the Beauty of the Description above.—+ Can you find any reason why we are invited to see this picture through the eyes of the interested and wondering Ichabod? Do you think the word *wondering* well chosen and suggestive? Look through this picture carefully and tell what there is that indicates thrift, industry, and prosperity. Find more common expressions for *center of the mansion* and *place of usual residence.* Notice in the third sentence the effect of *resplendent* and *dazzled.* How is a similar effect produced in the ninth and the tenth sentence? You see that this great artist in words does not here need to repeat his language. We can easily imagine that he could produce the same effect in a great variety of ways. In the fourth sentence does the expression *ready to be spun* tell what is actually seen, or what is only suggested? What is gained by this expression and by *just from the loom* in the next sentence? Do you think an unskillful artist would have used *in gay festoons?* Read the seventh and make it more common but less quaint. Do you think the picture gains, or loses, by representing the door as "ajar" instead of wide open? Why? Can you see any similar effect from introducing *their covert* in the tenth sentence? What does the expression *knowingly left open* suggest to you? This selection from Irving illustrates the +Descriptive+ style of writing.

SUGGESTIONS FOR COMPOSITION WORK.

In the description above we have taken some liberties with the original, for we have broken it up into single sentences. The parts of this picture as made by Irving were smoothly and delicately blended together.

You may rewrite this description; and, where it can be done to advantage, you may join the sentences neatly together. Perhaps some of these sentences may be changed to become parts of other sentences,

TO THE TEACHER.—It will be found profitable for pupils to break up for themselves into short sentences model selections from classic English, and, after examining the structure and style as suggested above, to note and, so far as possible, explain how these were blended together in the original. A written reproduction of the selection may then be made from memory.

This study of the thought, the structure, and the style of the great masters in language must lead to a discriminating taste for literature; and the effect upon the pupil's own habits of thought and expression will necessarily be to lift him above the insipid, commonplace matter and language that characterize much of the so-called "original" composition work.

In the study of these selections, especially in the work of copying, the rules for punctuation, and other rules, formally stated further on, may easily be anticipated informally.

For composition work more nearly original the class might read together or discuss, descriptions of home scenes; then, drawing from imagination or experience, they might make descriptions of their own. In these descriptions different persons might be introduced, with their attitudes, employments, and acts of hospitality.

For exercises in narration pupils might write about trips to these homes, telling about the preparation, the start, the journey, and the reception. (For studies on narrative style, see pages 157-162.)

To insure thoroughness, all such compositions should he short.

Exercises on the Composition of the Sentence and the Paragraph.

ADAPTED FROM IRVING'S "SKETCH BOOK."

1. Every window and crevice of the vast barn seemed bursting forth with the treasures of the farm. 2. The flail was busily resounding within from morning till night. 3. Swallows and martins skimmed twittering about the eaves. 4. Rows of pigeons were enjoying the sunshine on the roof. 5. Some sat with one eye turned up as if watching the weather. 6. Some sat with their heads under their wings or buried in their bosoms. 7. Others were swelling and cooing and bowing about their dames. 8. Sleek, unwieldy porkers were grunting in the repose and abundance of their pens. 9. From these pens sallied forth, now and then, troops of sucking pigs, as if to snuff the air. 10.

A stately squadron of snowy geese was riding in an adjoining pond, convoying whole fleets of ducks. 11. Regiments of turkeys were gobbling through the farmyard. 12. Guinea fowls fretted about, like ill-tempered housewives, with their peevish, discontented cry. 13. Before the barn-door strutted the gallant cock, clapping his burnished wings, and crowing in the pride and gladness of his heart—sometimes tearing up the earth with his feet, and then generously calling his ever-hungry family of wives and children to enjoy the rich morsel which he had discovered.

+The Uses of Words and Groups of Words+.—In the first sentence *seemed* asserts something about what two things? *Every* goes with what word or words? What word or words does the phrase *of the vast barn* make more definite in meaning? The two words *window* and *crevice* are joined together by what word? The group of words *bursting forth with the treasures of the farm* describes what? Notice that *bursting* also helps *seemed* to say something about window and crevice. *Seemed* does not make sense, but *seemed bursting* does. What does *forth* modify? What does *with the treasures of the farm* modify? In the third sentence what two nouns form the subject of *skimmed*? What connects these two nouns? In the fourth what word tells what the rows were enjoying? In the fifth *turned up as if watching the weather* describes what? *As if watching the weather* goes with what? The expression introduced by *as if* is a shortened form. Putting in some of the words omitted, we have *as if they were watching the weather. They were watching the weather*, if standing by itself, would make a complete sentence. You see that one sentence may be made a part of another sentence. What does each of the two phrases *under their wings* and *buried in their bosoms* describe? What connects these two phrases? In the seventh sentence *were* is understood before *cooing* and before *bowing*. How many predicate verbs do you find, each asserting something about the pigeons represented by *others*? Why are these verbs not separated by commas? What two nouns form the principal part of the phrase in the eighth sentence? What connects these two nouns? Read the ninth sentence and put the subject before the predicate. You may now explain *as if to snuff the air*, remembering that a similar expression in the fifth sentence was explained. In the tenth sentence *convoying whole fleets of ducks* describes what? Does *convoying* assert anything about the squadron? Change it into a predicate verb. In the twelfth sentence find one word and two phrases joined to *fretted. Clapping, crowing, tearing,* and *calling,* in the thirteenth, all describe what? Notice that all the other words following the subject go with these four. Find the three words that answer the questions made by putting *what* after *clapping, tearing, calling.* What phrase tells the cause of crowing? The phrase *to enjoy the rich morsel which he had discovered* tells the purpose of what? *Which he had discovered* limits the meaning of what? The pronoun *which* here stands for *morsel. Which he had discovered = He had discovered morsel.* Here you will see a sentence has again been made a part of another sentence. Notice that without *which* there would be no connection.

TO THE TEACHER.—It may be well to let the pupils complete the examination of the structure of the sentences above and point out nouns, verbs, pronouns, adjectives, and adverbs.

It will be noticed that in the questions above we especially anticipate the regular lessons that follow Lesson 27. This we do in all such "Exercises."

+The Beauty and the Force of the Description above+.—Why may we say that this farmyard scene is surrounded by an atmosphere of plenty, happiness, and content? Which do you prefer, the first sentence above, or this substitute for it: "The large barn was entirely full of the products of the farm"? Give every reason that you can find for your preference. We often speak of a barn or storehouse as "bursting with plenty," or of a table as "groaning with a load of good things," when there is really no bursting nor groaning. Such expressions are called +Figures of Speech+. Examine the second sentence and compare it with the following: "The men were busy all day pounding out the grain with flails." Do the words *busily resounding* joined to *flail* bring into our imagination men, grain, pounding, sound, and perhaps other things? A good description mentions such things and uses such words as will help us to see in imagination many things not mentioned. In the third sentence would you prefer *skimmed* to *flew*? Why? Compare the eighth sentence with this: "Large fat hogs were grunting in their pens and reposing quietly with an abundant supply of food." *Sleek, unwieldy porkers* would be too high-sounding an expression for you to use ordinarily, but it is in tone with the rest of the description. *In the repose and abundance of their pens* is much better than the words substituted above. It is shorter and stronger. It uses instead of the verb *reposing* and the adjective *abundant* the nouns *repose* and *abundance,* and makes these the principal words in the phrase. Repose and abundance are thus made the striking features of the pen. Arrange the ninth sentence in as many ways as possible and tell which way you prefer. Is a real squadron referred to in the tenth sentence? and were the geese actually convoying fleets? These are figurative uses of words. What can you say of *regiments* in the eleventh? In the twelfth Guinea fowls are compared to housewives. Except in this one fancied resemblance the two are wholly unlike. Such comparisons frequently made by *as* and *like* are called +Similes+. If we leave out *like* and say, "Guinea fowls are fretting housewives," we have a figure of speech called +Metaphor+. This figure is used above when flocks are called "squadrons" and "fleets." In the thirteenth sentence notice how well chosen and forceful are the words *strutted, gallant, burnished, generously, ever-hungry, rich morsel.* See whether you can find substitutes for these italicized words. Were the wings actually burnished? What can you say of this use of *burnished*?

SUGGESTIONS FOR COMPOSITION WORK.

The sentences in the description above, when read together, have a somewhat broken or jerky effect. You may unite smoothly such as should be joined. The fourth, fifth, sixth, and seventh can all be put into one. There is danger of making your sentences too long. Young writers find it difficult to make very long sentences perfectly clear in meaning.

TO THE TEACHER.—While the pupils' thoughts and style are somewhat toned up by the preceding exercises, it may he well to let them write similar descriptions drawn from their reading, their observation, or their imagination.

If the compositions contain more than two or three short paragraphs each, it will be almost impossible to secure good work.

Exercises on the Composition of the Sentence and the Paragraph.

FROM FRANKLIN'S "AUTOBIOGRAPHY."

1. I was dirty from my journey, my pockets were stuffed out with shirts and stockings, and I knew no soul nor where to look for lodging. 2. I was fatigued with traveling, rowing, and want of rest; I was very hungry; and my whole stock of cash consisted of a Dutch dollar and about a shilling in copper. 3. The latter I gave the people of the boat for my passage, who at first refused it on account of my rowing; but I insisted on their taking it.

1. Then I walked up the street, gazing about, till near the markethouse I met a boy with bread. 2. I had made many a meal on bread, and, inquiring where he got it, I went immediately to the baker's he directed me to, in Second Street, and asked for biscuit, intending such as we had in Boston; but they, it seems, were not made in Philadelphia. 3. Then I asked for a three-penny loaf, and was told they had none such. 4. So not considering or knowing the difference of money, or the greater cheapness and the names of

his bread, I bade him give me three-penny worth of any sort. 5. He gave me, accordingly, three great puffy rolls. 6. I was surprised at the quantity, but took it; and, having no room in my pockets, walked off with a roll under each arm, and eating the other.

* * * * *

+The Uses of Words and Groups of Words+.—Break up sentence 1, paragraph 1, into three distinct sentences, and tell what changes this will make in capitals and punctuation. Do the same for 2. Which read more closely together, and are more closely connected, the parts of 2, or of 1? How is this shown to the eye? Analyze the first two sentences you made from 1. Find two object complements of *knew*, one a noun and the other a group of five words. Find in 2 a phrase whose principal part is made up of three nouns. What have you learned about the commas used with these nouns? In making separate sentences of 3 what words do you change or drop? Are these the words that bind the parts of 3 together? What noun is used adverbially after *gave*? Supply a preposition and then tell what phrases modify *gave*. Find the object complement of *gave*. What modifies *refused* by telling when? What, by telling *why*?

In 1, paragraph 2, who is described as gazing about? What does *gazing about* modify? Read the group of words that tells how far or how long Franklin walked up the street. Notice that this whole group is used like an adverb. Find in it a subject, a predicate, and an object complement. Drop *till* and see whether the parts of 1 make separate sentences. What word, then, binds these two sentences into one? Read 2 and make of it three distinct sentences by omitting the first *and* and the word *but*. The second of these three sentences just made contains several sentences which are not so easily separated, as some are used like single words to make up the main, or principal, sentence. In this second part of 2 find the leading subject and its two predicates. Find a phrase belonging to *I* and representing Franklin as doing something. Put *what* after *inquiring* and find the object complement. What phrase belongs to *went,* telling where? *He directed me to (whom)* belongs to what? Who is represented as intending? *Intending such as we had in Boston* belongs to what? *As we had in Boston* goes with what? Notice that *it seems* is a sentence thrown in loosely between the parts of another sentence. Such expressions are said to be parenthetical. Notice the punctuation.

Notice that *gazing, inquiring, intending, considering, knowing,* and *having* are all modifiers of *I* found in the different sentences of paragraph 2. Put *I* before any one of these words, and you will see that no assertion is made. These words illustrate one form of the verb (the participle), and *look* in 1, paragraph 1, illustrates the other form (the infinitive), spoken of in Lesson 11 as not asserting. Change each of these participles to a predicate, or asserting form, and then read the sentences in which these predicates are found. You will notice that giving these words the asserting form makes them more prominent and forcible—brings them up to a level with the other predicate verbs. Participles are very useful in slurring over the less important actions that the more important may have prominence. Show that they are so used in Franklin's narrative.

Examine the phrase *with a roll under each arm, and eating the other,* and see if you do not find an illustration of the fact that even great men sometimes make slips. Does *other* properly mean one of three things? Try to improve this expression.

+The Grouping of Sentences into Paragraphs+.—The sentences above, as you see, stand in two groups. Those of each group are more closely related to one another than they are to the sentences of the other group. Do you see how? In studying this short selection you may find the general topic, or heading, to be something like this: *My First Experiences in Philadelphia.* Now examine the first group of sentences and see whether its topic might not be put thus: *My Condition on Reaching Philadelphia.* Then examine the sentences of the second group and see whether all will not come under this heading: *How I Found Something to Eat.* You see that even a short composition like this has a general topic with topics under it. As *sub* means *under,* we will call these under topics *sub-topics.* There are two groups of sentences in this selection because there are two distinct sub-topics developed. The sentences of each group stand together because they jointly develop one sub-topic.

A group of sentences related and held together by a common thought we call a +Paragraph+. How is the paragraph indicated to the eye? What help is it to the reader to have a composition paragraphed? What, to the writer to know that he must write in paragraphs?

+The Style of the Author+.—This selection is mainly +Narrative+. The matter is somewhat tame, and the expression is commonplace. The words are ordinary, and they stand in their usual place. Figures of speech are not used. Yet the piece has a charm. The thoughts are homely; the expression is in perfect keeping; the style is clear, simple, direct, and natural. The closing sentence is slightly humorous. Benjamin Franklin trudging along the street, hugging a great roll of bread under each arm, and eating a third roll, must have been a laughable sight.

Have you ever known boys and girls in writing school compositions, or reporters in writing for the newspapers, to use large words for small ideas, and long, high-sounding phrases and sentences for plain, simple thoughts? Have you ever seen what could be neatly said in three or four lines "padded out" to fill a page of composition paper or a column in a newspaper?

When Franklin said. "My pockets were stuffed out with shirts and stockings," he said a homely thing in a homely way; that is, he fitted the language to the thought. To fit the expression to the thought on every occasion is the perfection of style. If Franklin had been a weak, foolish writer, his sentence might have taken this form:—

"Not having been previously provided with a satchel or other receptacle for my personal effects, my pockets, which were employed as a substitute, were protruding conspicuously with extra underclothing."

Compare this sentence with Franklin's and point out the faults you see in the substitute. Can you find anything in the meaning of *provided* that makes previously unnecessary? Do you now understand what Lowell meant when, in praise of Dryden, he said, "His phrase is always a short cut to his sense"?

TO THE TEACHER.—What is here taught of the paragraph and of style will probably not be mastered at one reading. It will be found necessary to return to it occasionally, and to refer pupils to it for aid in their composition work.

SUGGESTIONS FOR COMPOSITION WORK.

TO THE TEACHER.—We suggest that the pupils reproduce from memory the extract above, and that other selections of narrative be found in the Readers or elsewhere and studied as above.

The pupils may be able to note to what extent the narrative follows the order of time and to what extent it is topical. They may also note the amount of description it contains. They should, so far as possible, find the topic for each paragraph, thus making an outline for a composition to be completed from reproduction.

It will now require little effort to write simple original narratives of real or imagined experiences.

* * * * *

Exercises on the Composition of the Sentence and the Paragraph.

FROM C. D. WARNER'S "MY SUMMER IN A GARDEN."

1. In the driest days, my fountain became disabled; the pipe was stopped up. 2. A couple of plumbers, with the implements of their craft, came out to view the situation. 3. There was a good deal of difference of opinion about where the stoppage was. 4. I found the plumbers perfectly willing to sit down and talk about it—talk by the hour. 5. Some of their guesses and remarks were exceedingly ingenious; and their general observations on other subjects were excellent in their way, and could hardly have been better if they had been made by the job. 6. The work dragged a little—as it is apt to do by the hour.

1. The plumbers had occasion to make me several visits. 2. Sometimes they would find, upon arrival, that they had forgotten some indispensable tool; and one would go back to the shop, a mile and a half, after it; and his comrade would await his return with the most exemplary patience, and sit down and talk—always by the hour. 3. I do not know but it is a habit to have something wanted at the shop. 4. They seemed to me very good workmen, and always willing to stop, and talk about the job or anything else, when I went near them. 5. Nor had they any of that impetuous hurry that is said to be the bane of our American civilization. 6. To their credit be it said that I never observed anything of it in them. 7. They can afford to wait. 8. Two of them will sometimes wait nearly half a day, while a comrade goes for a tool. 9. They are patient and philosophical. 10. It is a

great pleasure to meet such men. 11. One only wishes there was some work he could do for them by the hour.

+The Uses of Words and Groups of Words+.—How can you make the last part of 1 express more directly the cause of becoming disabled? Would you use a semicolon to separate the sentences thus joined, or would you use a comma? Give a reason for the comma after *days*, Find in 2 an adverb phrase that expresses purpose. Use an equivalent adjective in place of *a couple of*. Explain the use of *there* in 3. What adjective may be used in place of *good* in *a good deal*? What long complex phrase modifies *deal*? Put *what* after the preposition *about* and find a group of words that takes the place of a noun. Find in this group a subject and a predicate. Find in 4 an objective complement. Find a compound infinitive phrase and tell what it modifies. Notice that the dash helps to show the break made by repeating *talk*. When 5 is divided into two sentences, what word is dropped? This, then, must be the word that connected the two sentences. Notice that the two main parts of 5 are separated by a semicolon. This enables the writer to show that the two main divisions of 5 are more widely separated in meaning than are the parts of the second division where the comma is used. Give the three leading predicate verbs in 5 and their complements. *If they had been made by the job* is joined like an adverb to what verb? What is the predicate of this modifying group?

The infinitive phrase in 1, paragraph 2, modifies what? Is *me*, or *visits*, the object complement of *make*? Put *what* after *would find* in 2 and get the object complement. Can you make a sentence of this group? What are its principal parts? Does the writer make an unexpected turn after *talk*? How is this shown to the eye? Put *what* after *do know* in 3 and find the object complement. Can you make a sentence of this object complement? What phrase can you put in place of the pronoun *it* without changing the sense? By using the word *it*, a better arrangement can be made. What group of words in 5 is used like an adjective to modify *hurry*? Change the pronoun *that* to *hurry* and make a separate sentence of this group. What word, then, must have made an adjective of this sentence and joined it to *hurry*? What is the object complement of *can afford* in 7? Supply a preposition after *will wait* in 8, and then find two groups of words that tell the time of waiting. Find a subject and a predicate in the second group. What explains *it* in 10? Find the object complement of *wishes* in 11. What is the subject of *was*? The office of *there*? After *work* supply the pronoun *that* and tell the office of the group it introduces. What is the object complement of *could do*? What connects this group to *work*?

+The Grouping of Sentences into Paragraphs+.—There are two distinct sets of sentences in this selection—distinct because developing two distinct sub-topics. Accordingly, there are two paragraphs. Let us take for the general topic *The Visits of the Plumbers*. Let us see whether all the sentences of the first paragraph will not come under the sub-topic *First Visit*, and those of the second under the sub-topic *Subsequent Visits*. The sentences of each paragraph should be closely related to one another and to the sub-topic. They should stand in their proper order. Do the paragraphs above stand such tests? If they do, they possess the prime quality of +Unity+.

+The Author's Style+.—This selection we may call +Narrative+, though there are descriptive touches in it. It is a story of what? Is the story clearly told throughout? If not, where is it obscure? Is it made interesting and entertaining? Is Mr. Warner here giving us a bit of his own experience? Or do you think he is drawing upon his imagination? Would you call the style plain, or does it abound with metaphors, similes, or other figures of speech? Are the sentences generally long, or generally short? What are the faults or

In what sentence is the style made +energetic+ by the aid of short predicates? How does the alternation of short sentences with long throughout the extract affect you? The alternation of plain with figurative sentences? Can you show that the author's style has +Variety+? Pick out the metaphors in 1, 2, 3, and 5, paragraph 2; and in 1 and 2, paragraph 3. Pick out the comparisons, or similes, in 3, paragraph 1, and in 3, paragraph 2. Figures of speech should add clearness and force. If you think these do, tell how. *Indolence* in 1 and 3, paragraph 2, and *laziness* in 2, introduce us to another figure. Something belonging to the men, a quality, is made to represent the men themselves. Such a figure is called +Metonymy+.

SUGGESTIONS FOB COMPOSITION WORK.

TO THE TEACHER.—Exercises in argumentative writing may be continued by making selections from the discussion of easy topics.

For original work we suggest debates on current topics. Compositions should be short.

Exercises on the Composition of the Sentence and the Paragraph.

EXTRACT FROM DANIEL WEBSTER.

1. The assassin enters, through the window already prepared, into an unoccupied apartment. 2. With noiseless foot he paces the lonely hall, half lighted by the moon; he winds up the ascent of the stairs and reaches the door of the chamber. 3. Of this he moves the lock, by soft and continued pressure, till it turns on its hinges without noise; and he enters, and beholds his victim before him.

1. The face of the innocent sleeper is turned from the murderer, and the beams of the moon, resting on the gray locks of his aged temple, show him where to strike. 2. The fatal blow is given! and the victim passes, without a struggle or a motion, from the repose of sleep to the repose of death. 3. It is the assassin's purpose to make sure work; and he plies the dagger, though it is obvious that life has been destroyed by the blow of the bludgeon. 4. He even raises the aged arm that he may not fail in his aim at the heart, and places it again over the wounds of the poniard. 5. To finish the picture, he explores the wrist for the pulse. 6. He feels for it, and ascertains that it beats no longer. 7. It is accomplished. 8. The deed is done.

1. He retreats, retraces his steps to the window, passes out through it as he came in, and escapes. 2. He has done the murder. No eye has seen him, no ear has heard him. 3. The secret is his own, and it is safe.

1. Ah! gentlemen, that was a dreadful mistake. 2. Such a secret can be safe nowhere. 3. The whole creation of God has neither nook nor corner where the guilty can bestow it, and say it is safe. 4. Not to speak of that eye which pierces through all disguises and beholds everything as in the splendor of noon, such secrets of guilt are never safe from detection even by men. 5. True it is, generally speaking, that "Murder will out." 6. True it is that Providence hath so ordained, and doth so govern things, that those who break the great law of heaven by shedding man's blood seldom succeed in avoiding discovery.

* * * * *

+The Uses of Words and Groups of Words+.—Do the phrases in 1, paragraph 1, stand in their usual order, or are they transposed? In what different places may they stand? Does either phrase need to be transposed for emphasis or for clearness? Explain the punctuation. Begin 2 with *the lonely hall*, and notice that the sentence is thrown out of harmony with the other sentences, and that the assassin is for the moment lost sight of. Can you tell why? Notice that in the latter part of 2 the door is mentioned, and that 3 begins with *of this*, referring to the door. Can you find any other arrangement by which 3 will follow 2 so naturally? Can you change 3 so as to make the reference of *it* clearer? What is the office of the *till* clause? Does the clause following the semicolon modify anything? Would you call such a clause *dependent*, or would you call it *independent*? Explain the punctuation of 3.

Give the effect of changing *resting* in 1, paragraph 2, to the assertive form. Find in 1 a pronoun used adverbially and a phrase used as object complement. Expand the phrase into a clause. Give the modifiers of *passes* in 2. Read the first part of 3 and put the explanatory phrase in place of *it*. What is the office of the *though* clause? Find in this a clause doing the work of a noun and tell its office. In 4 would *his* in place of *the* before *aged* and before *heart* be ambiguous? If so, why? Find in this paragraph an infinitive phrase used independently. Find the object complement of *ascertains* in 6. Are 7 and 8 identical in meaning?

Give the modifiers of *passes* in paragraph 3. Explain the *as* clause. What does *that* in 1, paragraph 4, stand for? What kind of clause is introduced by *where* in 3? By *which* in 4? Expand the *as* clause in 4 and tell its office. Find in 4 and 5 an infinitive phrase and a participle phrase used independently. Tell the office of the *that* clauses in 5 and 6, and of the *who* clause in 6.

+The Grouping of Sentences into Paragraphs+.—Look (1) at the order of the sentences in each paragraph, and (2) at the order of the paragraphs themselves. Neither order could be changed without making the stream of events run up hill, for each order is the order in which the events happened. Look (3) at the unity of each paragraph, and (4) at the larger unity of the four paragraphs—that of each paragraph determined by the relation of each sentence to the sub-topic of the paragraph, and that of the four paragraphs determined by their relation to the general topic of the extract. We add that the obvious reference of the repeated *he* to the same person, and of *that* and *secret* in paragraph 4 demonstrates both unities. Look (5), and lastly, at the fact that the sub-topic of each paragraph is found in the first line of each paragraph. Could Webster have done more to make his thought seen and felt?

+The Style of the Author.+—This selection is largely +Narrative.+ Its leading facts were doubtless supplied by the testimony given in the case; but much of the matter must have come from the imagination of Mr. Webster. Everything is so skillfully and vividly put that the story, touched with description, has all the effect of an argument. One quality of it is its clearness, its perspicuity. It is noticeable also that very little imagery is used, that the language is plain language. But it is impossible to read these paragraphs without being most profoundly impressed with their energy, their force.

The style is forcible because (1) the +subject-matter+ is +easily grasped+; (2) because +simple words+ are +used+, words understood even by children; because (3) these +words+ are +specific+ and +individual+, not generic; because (4) of the grateful +variety of sentences+; (5) because of the +prevalence of short sentences+; because (6) of the +repetition of the thought+ in successive sentences; because (7), though the murder took place some time before, Webster speaks as if it were +now taking place+ in our very sight. Find proof of what we have just said—proof of (2), in paragraphs 1 and 3; proof of (3), in sentences 3, 4, and 5, paragraph 2; proof of (4), throughout; of (5) and (6), in paragraphs 3 and 4; and of (7), in the first three paragraphs.

In paragraph 3, a remarkable sameness prevails. The sentences here are framed largely on one plan. They are mostly of the same length. The order of the words in them is the same; often the words are the same; and, even when they are not, those in one clause or sentence seem to suggest those in the next. This sameness is not accidental. The more real the murderer's fancied security is made in this paragraph to appear, the more startling in the next paragraph will be the revelation of his mistake. Hence no novelty in the words or in their arrangement is allowed to distract our attention from the dominant thought. The sentences are made to look and sound alike and to be alike that their effect may be cumulative. The principle of +Parallel Construction+, the principle that sentences similar in thought should be similar in form, is here allowed free play.

TO THE TEACHER.—Do not be discouraged should your pupils fail to grasp at first all that is here taught. They probably will not fully comprehend it till they have returned to it several times. It will, however, be impossible for them to study it without profit. The meaning will grow upon them. In studying our questions and suggestions the pupils should have the "Extract" before them, and should try to verify in it all that is taught concerning it.

* * * * *

PARTS OF SPEECH SUBDIVIDED

LESSON 85.

CLASSES OF NOUNS AND PRONOUNS.

+Introductory Hints+.—You have now reached a point where it becomes necessary to divide the eight great classes of words into subclasses.

You have learned that nouns are the names of things; as, *girl*, *Sarah*. The name *girl* is held in common by all girls, and hence does not distinguish one girl from another. The name *Sarah* is not thus held in common; it does distinguish one girl from other girls. Any name which belongs in common to all things of a class we call a +Common Noun+; and any particular name of an individual, distinguishing this individual from others of its class, we call a +Proper Noun+. The "proper, or individual, names" which in Rule 1, Lesson 8, you were told to begin with capital letters are proper nouns.

Such a word as *wheat, music,* or *architecture* does not distinguish one thing from others of its class; there is but one thing in the class denoted by each, each thing forms a class by itself; and so we call these words common nouns.

In Lesson 8 you learned that pronouns are not names, but words used instead of names. Any one speaking of himself may use *I, my*, etc., instead of his own name; speaking to one, he may use *you, thou, your, thy*, etc., instead of that person's name; speaking of one, he may use *he, she, it, him, her*, etc., instead of that one's name. These little words that by their form denote the speaker, the one spoken to, or the one spoken of are called +Personal Pronouns+.

By adding *self* to *my, thy, your, him, her,* and *it*, and *selves* to *our, your,* and *them*, we form what are called +Compound Personal Pronouns+, used either for emphasis or to reflect the action of the verb back upon the actor; as, *Xerxes himself* was the last to cross the Hellespont; The *mind* cannot see *itself*.

If a noun, or some word or words used like a noun, is to be modified by a clause, the clause is introduced by *who, which, what,* or *that*; as, I know the man *that* did that. These words, relating to words in another clause, and binding the clauses together, are called +Relative Pronouns+. By adding *ever* and *soever* to *who, which*, and *what*, we form what are called the +Compound Relative Pronouns+ *whoever, whosoever, whichever, whatever*, etc., used in a general way, and without any word expressed to which they relate.

If the speaker is ignorant of the name of a person or a thing and asks for it, he uses *who, which*, or *what*; as, *Who* did that? These pronouns, used in asking questions, are called +Interrogative Pronouns+.

Instead of naming things a speaker may indicate them by words pointing them out as near or remote; as, Is *that* a man? What is *this*? or by words telling something of their number, order, or quantity; as, *None* are perfect; The *latter* will do; *Much* has been done. Such words we call +Adjective Pronouns+.

DEFINITIONS.

+A *Noun* is the name of anything+. [Footnote: Most common nouns are derived from roots that denote qualities. The root does not necessarily denote the most essential quality of the thing, only its most obtrusive quality. The sky, a shower, and scum, for instance, have this most noticeable feature; they are a cover, they hide, conceal. This the root +sku+ signifies, and *sku* is the main element in the words *sky, shower* (Saxon *scu:r*), and *scum* that name these objects, and in the adjective *obscure*.

A noun denoting at first only a single quality of its object comes gradually, by the association of this quality with the rest, to denote them all.

Herein proper nouns differ from common. However derived, as *Smith* is from the man's office of smoothing, or *White* from his color, the name soon ceases to denote quality, and becomes really meaningless.]

+A *Common Noun* is a name which belongs to all things of a class+.

+A *Proper Noun* is the particular name of an individual+.

+Remark+.—It may be well to note two classes of common nouns—*collective* and *abstract*. A +Collective Noun+ is the name of a number of things taken together; as, *army, flock, mob, jury*. An +Abstract Noun+ is the name of a quality, an action, a being, or a state; as, *whiteness, beauty, wisdom,* (the) *singing, existence,* (the) *sleep*.

+A *Pronoun* is a word used for a noun+. [Footnote: In our definition and general treatment of the pronoun, we have conformed to the traditional views of grammarians; but it may be well for the student to note that pronouns are something more than mere substitutes for nouns, and that their primary function is not to prevent the repetition of nouns.

1. Pronouns are not the names of things. They do not, like nouns, lay hold of qualities and name things by them. They seize upon relations that objects sustain to each other and denote the objects by these relations. *I, you,* and *he* denote their objects by the relations these objects sustain to the act of speaking; *I* denotes the speaker; *you,* the one spoken to; and *he* or *she* or *it,* the one spoken of. *This* and *that* denote their objects by the relative distance of these from the speaker; *some* and *few* and *others* indicate parts separated from the rest. Gestures could express all that many pronouns express.

2. It follows that pronouns are more general than nouns. Any person, or even an animal or a thing personified, may use *I* when referring to himself, *you* when referring to the one addressed, and *he, she, it,* and *they* when referring to the person or persons, the thing or things, spoken of—and all creatures and things, except the speaker and the one spoken to, fall into the last list. Some pronouns are so general, and hence so vague, in their

denotement that they show the speaker's complete ignorance of the objects they denote. In, *Who* did it? *Which* of them did you see? the questioner is trying to find out the one for whom *Who* stands, and the person or thing that *Which* denotes. To what does *it* refer in, *it* rains; How is *it* with you?

3. Some pronouns stand for a phrase, a clause, or a sentence, going before or coming after. *To be* or *not to be—that* is the question. *It is doubtful whether the North Pole will ever be reached. The sails turned, the corn was ground,* after *which* the wind ceased. *Ought you to go?* I cannot answer *that*. In the first of these sentences, *that* stands for a phrase; in the last, for a sentence. *It* and *which* in the second and third sentences stand for clauses.

4. *Which*, retaining its office as connective, may as an adjective accompany its noun; as, I craved his forbearance a little longer, *which forbearance* he allowed me.]

+A *Personal Pronoun* is a pronoun that by its form denotes the speaker, the one spoken to, or the one spoken of+.

+A *Relative Pronoun* is one that relates to some preceding word or words and connects clauses+.

+An *Interrogative Pronoun* is one with which a question is asked+.

+An *Adjective Pronoun* is one that performs the offices of both an adjective and a noun+.

The simple personal pronouns are:—*I, thou, you, he, she,* and *it.*

The compound personal pronouns are:—*Myself, thyself, yourself, himself, herself,* and *itself.*

The simple relative pronouns are:—*Who, which, that,* and *what.* [Footnote: *As,* in such sentences as this: Give such things *as* you can spare, may be treated as a relative pronoun. But by expanding the sentence *as* is seen to be a conjunctive adverb—Give such things *as those are which* you can spare.

But used after a negative is sometimes called a "negative relative" = *that not;* as, There is not a man here *but* would die for such a cause. When the sentence is expanded, *but* is found to be a preposition—There is not a man here *but* (= *except*) the one who would die, etc.]

The compound relative pronouns are:—

Whoever or *whosoever, whichever* or *whichsoever, whatever* or *whatsoever.*

The interrogative pronouns are:—

Who, which, and *what.*

Some of the more common adjective pronouns are:—

All, another, any, both, each, either, enough, few, former, latter, little, many, much, neither, none, one, other, same, several, such, that, these, this, those, whole, etc. [Footnote: The adjective pronouns *this, that, these,* and *those* are called +Demonstrative+ pronouns. *All, any, both, each, either, many, one, other,* etc. are called +Indefinite+ pronouns because they do not point out and particularize like the demonstratives. *Each, either,* and *neither* are also called +Distributives+.

But for the fact that such words as *brave, good,* etc. in the phrases *the brave, the good,* etc. describe—which pronouns never do—we might call them adjective pronouns. They may be treated as nouns, or as adjectives modifying nouns to be supplied.

Some adjectives preceded by *the* are abstract nouns; as, the *grand*, the *sublime*, the *beautiful*.]

The word, phrase, or clause in the place of which a pronoun is used is called an +Antecedent+.

+Direction+.—*Point out the pronouns and their antecedents in these sentences*:—

Jack was rude to Tom, and always knocked off his hat when he met him. To lie is cowardly, and every boy should know it. Daniel and his companions were fed on pulse, which was to their advantage. To lie is to be a coward, which one should scorn to be. To sleep soundly, which is a blessing, is to repair and renew the body.

+Remark+.—When the interrogatives *who, which,* and *what* introduce indirect questions, it is not always easy to distinguish them from relatives whose antecedents are omitted. For example—I found *who* called and *what* he wanted; I saw *what* was done. The first sentence does not mean, I found the *person who* called and the *thing that* he wanted. "*Who* called" and "*what* he wanted" here suggest questions—questions referred to but not directly asked. I saw *what* was done = I saw the *thing that* was done. No question is suggested.

It should be remembered that *which* and *what* may also be interrogative adjectives; as, *Which* side won? *What* news have you?

+Direction+.—*Analyze these sentences, and parse all the pronouns*:—

1. Who steals my purse steals trash. 2. I myself know who stole my purse. 3. They knew whose house was robbed. 4. He heard what was said. 5. You have guessed which belongs to me. 6. Whom the gods would destroy they first make mad. 7. What was said, and who said it? 8. It is not known to whom the honor belongs. 9. She saw one of them, but she cannot positively tell which. 10. Whatever is done must be done quickly.

* * * * *

LESSON 86.

CONSTRUCTION OF PRONOUNS.

TO THE TEACHER.—In the recitation of all Lessons containing errors for correction, the pupils' books should be closed, and the examples should be read by you. To insure care in preparation, and close attention in the class, read some of the examples in their correct form. Require specific reasons.

+Caution+.—Avoid *he, it, they*, or any other pronoun when its reference to an antecedent would not be clear. Repeat the noun instead, quote the speaker's exact words, or recast the sentence.

+Direction+.—*Study the Caution, and relieve these sentences of their ambiguity:*—

+Model+.—The lad cannot leave his father; for, if he should leave *him, he* would die = The lad cannot leave his father; for, if he should leave *his father, his father* would die. Lysias promised his father never to abandon *his* friends = Lysias gave his father this promise: "I will never abandon *your* (or *my*) friends."

1. Dr. Prideaux says that, when he took his commentary to the bookseller, he told him it was a dry subject.
2. He said to his friend that, if he did not feel better soon, he thought he had better go home.

(This sentence may have four meanings. Give them all, using what you may suppose were the speaker's words.)

3. A tried to see B in the crowd, but could not because he was so short. 4. Charles's duplicity was fully made known to Cromwell by a letter of his to his wife, which he intercepted. 5. The farmer told the lawyer that his bull had gored his ox, and that it was but fair that he should pay him for his loss.

+Caution+.—Do not use pronouns needlessly.

+Direction+.—*Write, these sentences, omitting needless pronouns:*—

1. It isn't true what he said. 2. The father he died, the mother she followed, and the children they were taken sick. 3. The cat it mewed, and the dogs they barked, and the man he shouted. 4. Let every one turn from his or her evil ways. 5. Napoleon, Waterloo having been lost, he gave himself up to the English.

+Caution+.—In addressing a person, do not, in the same sentence, use the two styles of the pronoun.

+Direction+.—*Study the Caution, and correct these errors:*—

1. Thou art sad, have you heard bad news? 2. You cannot always have thy way. 3. Bestow thou upon us your blessing. 4. Love thyself last, and others will love you.

+Caution+.—The pronoun *them* should not be used for the adjective *those*, nor the pronoun *what* for the conjunction *that*. [Footnote: *What* properly introduces a noun clause expressing a direct or an indirect question, but a declarative noun clause is introduced by the conjunction *that*. *But* may be placed before this conjunction to give a negative force to the noun clause.

This use of *but* requires careful discrimination. For example—"I have no fear *that* he will do it"; "I have no fear *but that* he will do it." The former indicates certainty that he will not do it, and the latter certainty that he will do it. "No one doubts but that he will do it" is incorrect, for it contains three negatives—*no, doubts*, and *but*. Two negatives may be used to affirm, but not three. The intended meaning is, "*No* one *doubts* that he will do it," or "*No* one believes *but* that he will do it," or "Every one *believes* that he will do it."

But what, for *but that* or *but*, is also incorrectly used to connect an adverb clause; as, "He is not so bad *but what* he might be worse." For this office of *but* or *but that* in an adverb clause, see Lesson 109, fourth "Example" of the uses of *but*.]

+Direction+.—*Study the Caution, and correct these errors*:—

1. Hand me them things. 2. Who knows but what we may fail? 3. I cannot believe but what I shall see them men again. 4. We ought to have a great regard for them that are wise and good.

+Caution+.—The relative *who* should always represent persons; *which*, brute animals and inanimate things; *that*, persons, animals, and things; and *what*, things. The antecedent of *what* should not be expressed.

+Direction+.—*Study the Caution, and correct these errors*:—

1. Those which say so are mistaken. 2. He has some friends which I know. 3. He told that what he knew. 4. The dog who was called Fido went mad. 5. The lion whom they were exhibiting broke loose. 6. All what he saw he described. 7. The horse whom Alexander rode was named Bucephalus.

+Direction+.—*Write correct sentences illustrating every point in these five Cautions.*

LESSON 87.

CONSTRUCTION OF PRONOUNS—CONTINUED.

+Caution+.—Several connected relative clauses relating to the same antecedent require the same relative pronoun.

+Direction+.—*Study the Caution, and correct these errors:*—

1. It was Joseph that was sold into Egypt, who became governor of the land, and which saved his father and brothers from famine. 2. He who lives, that moves, and who has his being in God should not forget him. 3. This is the horse which started first, and that reached the stand last. 4. The man that fell overboard, and who was drowned was the first mate.

+Caution+.—When the relative clause is not restrictive, [Footnote: See Lesson 61.] *who* or *which*, and not *that*, is generally used.

+Example+.—Water, *which* is composed of hydrogen and oxygen, covers three-fourths of the earth's surface.

+Direction+.—*Study the Caution, and correct these errors:*—

1. The earth is enveloped by an ocean of air, that is a compound of oxygen. and nitrogen. 2. Longfellow, that is the most popular American poet, has written beautiful prose. 3. Time, that is a precious gift, should not be wasted. 4. Man, that is born of woman, is of few days and full of trouble.

+Caution+.—The relative *that* [Footnote: *That* is almost always restrictive. However desirable it may seem to confine *who* and *which* to unrestrictive clauses, they are not confined to them in actual practice.

The wide use of *who* and *which* in restrictive clauses is not accounted for by saying that they occur after *this, these, those,* and *that,* and hence are used to avoid disagreeable repetitions of sounds. This may frequently be the reason for employing *who* and *which* in restrictive clauses; but usage authorizes us to affirm (1) that *who* and *which* stand in such clauses oftener without, than with, *this, these, those,* or *that* preceding them, and (2) that they so stand oftener than *that* itself does. Especially may this be said of *which*.] should be used instead of *who* or *which* (1) when the antecedent names both persons and things; (2) when *that* would prevent ambiguity; and (3) when it would sound better than *who* or *which, e. g.,* after *that, same, very, all,* the interrogative *who,* the indefinite *it,* and adjectives expressing quality in the highest degree.

+Example+.—He lived near a *pond that* was a nuisance. (*That* relates to *pond*—the pond was a nuisance. *Which* might have, for its antecedent, *pond,* or the whole clause *He lived near a pond*; and so its use here would be ambiguous.)

+Direction+.—*Study the Caution, and correct these errors:*—

1. The wisest men who ever lived made mistakes. 2. The chief material which is used now in building is brick. 3. Who who saw him did not pity him? 4. He is the very man whom we want. 5. He is the same who he has

ever been. 6. He sent his boy to a school which did him good. 7. All who knew him respected him. 8. It was not I who did it. 9. That man that you just met is my friend.

+Caution+.—The relative clause should be placed as near as possible to the word which it modifies.

+Direction+.—*Correct these errors*:—

1. The pupil will receive a reward from his teacher who is diligent. 2. Her hair hung in ringlets, which was dark and glossy. 3. A dog was found in the street that wore a brass collar. 4. A purse was picked up by a boy that was made of leather. 5. Claudius was canonized among the gods, who scarcely deserved the name of man. 6. He should not keep a horse that cannot ride.

+Caution+.—When *this* and *that*, *these* and *those*, *the one* and *the other* refer to things previously mentioned, *this* and *these* refer to the last mentioned, and *that* and *those* to the first mentioned; *the one* refers to the first mentioned, and *the other* to the last mentioned. When there is danger of obscurity, repeat the nouns.

+Examples+.—*High* and *tall* are synonyms: *this* may be used in speaking of what grows—a tree; *that*, in speaking of what does not grow—a mountain. Homer was a genius; Virgil, an artist: in *the one* we most admire the man; in *the other*, the work.

+Direction+.—*Study the Caution, and correct these errors*:—

1. Talent speaks learnedly at the bar; tact, triumphantly: this is complimented by the bench; that gets the fees.
2. Charles XII. and Peter the Great were sovereigns: the one was loved by his people; the other was hated.

3. The selfish and the benevolent are found in every community; these are shunned, while those are sought after.

+Direction+.—*Write correct sentences illustrating every point in these five Cautions.*

* * * * *

LESSON 88.

CONSTRUCTION OF PRONOUNS—CONTINUED.

Miscellaneous Errors.

+Direction+.—*Give the Cautions which these sentences violate, and correct the errors*:—

1. He who does all which he can does enough. 2. John's father died before he was born. 3. Whales are the largest animals which swim. 4. Boys who study hard, and that study wisely make progress. 5. There are miners that live below ground, and who seldom see the light. 6. He did that what was right. 7. General Lee, that served under Washington, had been a British officer. 8. A man should sit down and count the cost who is about to build a house. 9. They need no spectacles that are blind. 10. They buy no books who are not able to read. 11. Cotton, that is a plant, is woven into cloth. 12. Do you know that gentleman that is speaking? 13. There is no book which, when we look through it sharply, we cannot find mistakes in it. 14. The reporter which said that was deceived. 15. The diamond, that is pure carbon, is a brilliant gem. 16. The brakemen and the cattle which were on the train were killed. 17. *Reputation* and *character* do not mean the same thing: the one denotes what we are; the other, what we are thought to be. 18. Kosciusko having come to this country, he aided us in our Revolutionary struggle. 19. What pleased me much, and which was spoken of by others,

was the general appearance of the class. 20. There are many boys whose fathers and mothers died when they were infants. 21. Witness said that his wife's father came to his house, and he ordered him out, but he refused to go. 22. Shall you be able to sell them boots? 23. I don't know but what I may. 24. Beer and wine are favorite drinks abroad: the one is made from grapes; the other, from barley. 25. There is one marked difference between shiners and trout; these have scales, and those have not. 26. They know little of men, who reason thus. 27. Help thyself, and Heaven will help you.

* * * * *

LESSON 89.

CLASSES OF ADJECTIVES.

+Introductory Hints+.—You learned in Lesson 12 that, in the sentences *Ripe apples are healthful, Unripe apples are hurtful*, the adjectives *ripe* and *unripe* limit, or narrow, the application of *apples* by describing, or by expressing certain qualities of the fruit. You learned also that *the, this, an, no, some*, and *many* limit, or narrow, the application of any noun which they modify, as *apple* or *apples*, by pointing out the particular fruit, by numbering it, or by denoting the quantity of it.

Adjectives which limit by expressing quality are called +Descriptive Adjectives+; and those which limit by pointing out, numbering, or denoting quantity are called +Definitive Adjectives+.

Adjectives modifying a noun do not limit, or narrow, its application (1) when they denote qualities that always belong to the thing named; as, *yellow* gold, the *good* God, the *blue* sky; or (2) when they are attribute complements, denoting qualities asserted by the verb; as, The fields were *green*; The ground was *dry* and *hard*.

+DEFINITIONS+.

+An *Adjective* is a word used to modify a noun or a pronoun+.[Footnote: Pronouns, like nouns, are often modified by an "appositive" adjective, that is, an adjective joined loosely without restricting: thus—*Faint* and *weary, he* struggled on or, *He, faint* and *weary,* struggled on. Adjectives that complete the predicate belong as freely to pronouns as to nouns.]

+A *Descriptive Adjective* is one that modifies by expressing quality+.

+A *Definitive Adjective* is one that modifies by pointing out, numbering, or denoting quantity+.[Footnote: The definitive adjectives *one, two, three,* etc.; *first, second, third,* etc. are called +Numeral+ adjectives. *One, two, three,* etc. are called +Cardinal+ numerals; and *first, second, third*—etc. are called +Ordinal+ numerals]

The definitive adjectives *an* or *a* and *the* are commonly called +Articles+. *An* or *a* is called the *Indefinite Article,* and *the* is called the *Definite Article.*

A noun may take the place of an adjective.

+Examples+.—*London* journals, the *New York* press, *silver* spoons, *diamond* pin, *state* papers, *gold* bracelet.

+Direction+.—*Point out the descriptive and the definitive adjectives below, and name such as do not limit:—*

Able statesmen, much rain, ten mice, brass kettle, small grains, Mansard roof, some feeling, all men, hundredth anniversary, the Pitt diamond, the patient Hannibal, little thread, crushing argument, moving spectacle, the martyr president, tin pans, few people, less trouble, this toy, any book, brave Washington, Washington market, three cats, slender cord, that libel, happy children, the broad Atlantic, The huge clouds were dark and threatening, Eyes are bright, What name was given? Which book is wanted?

+Direction+.—*Point out the descriptive and the definitive adjectives in Lessons 80 and 81, and tell whether they denote color, motion, shape, position, size, moral qualities, or whether they modify in some other way.*

* * * * *

LESSON 90.

CONSTRUCTION OF ADJECTIVES.

+Caution+.—*An* and *a* are different forms of *one*. *An* is used before vowel sounds. For the sake of euphony, *an* drops *n* and becomes *a* before consonant sounds.[Footnote: Some writers still use *an* before words beginning with unaccented *h*; as, *an historian*.]

+Examples+.—*An* inkstand, *a* bag, *a* historian, *a* humble petition, *an* hour (*h* is silent), *a* unit (*unit* begins with the consonant sound of *y*), such *a* one (*one* begins with the consonant sound of *w*). +Direction+.—*Study the Caution, and correct these errors:*—

A heir, a inheritance, an hook, an ewer, an usurper, a account, an uniform, an hundred, a umpire, an hard apple, an hero.

+Caution.+—*An* or *a* is used to limit a noun to one thing of a class—to any one. *The* is used to distinguish (1) one thing or several things from others, and (2) one class of things from other classes.

+Explanation.+—We can say *a horse*, meaning *any one horse*; but we cannot say, *A gold* is heavy, This is a poor kind of a *gas*, William Pitt received the title of *an earl* because *gold*, *gas*, and *earl* are here meant to denote each the whole of a class, and *a* limits its noun to one thing of a class.

The horse or *the horses* must be turned into *the lot*. Here *the* before *horse* distinguishes a certain animal, and the before horses distinguishes certain animals, from others of the same class; and *the* before *lot* distinguishes the field from the yard or the stable—things in other classes. *The horse* is a noble animal. Here *the* distinguishes *this class* of animals from other classes. But we cannot say, The man (meaning the race) is mortal, *The anger* is a short madness, *The truth* is eternal, *The poetry* and *the painting* are fine arts, because *man, anger, truth, poetry,* and *painting* are used in their widest sense, and name things that are sufficiently distinguished without *the*.

+Direction.+—*Study the Caution as explained, and correct these errors*:—

1. This is another kind of a sentence. 2. Churchill received the title of a duke. 3. A *hill* is from the same root as *column*. 4. Dog is a quadruped. 5. I expected some such an offer. 6. The woman is the equal of man. 7. The sculpture is a fine art. 8. Unicorn is kind of a rhinoceros. 9. Oak is harder than the maple.

+Caution.+—Use *an, a,* or *the* before *each* of two or more connected adjectives, when these adjectives modify different nouns, expressed or understood; but, when they modify the same noun, the article should not be repeated.

+Explanation+.—*A cotton and a silk umbrella* means two umbrellas—one cotton and the other silk; the word umbrella is understood after *cotton*. *A cotton and silk umbrella* means one umbrella partly cotton and partly silk;

cotton and *silk* modify the same noun—*umbrella*. *The wise and the good* means two classes; *the wise and good* means one class.

+Direction+.—*Study the Caution as explained, and correct these errors*:—

1. The Northern and Southern Hemisphere. 2. The Northern and the Southern Hemispheres. 3. The right and left hand. 4. A Pullman and Wagner sleeping-coach. 5. The fourth and the fifth verses. 6. The fourth and fifth verse. 7. A Webster's and Worcester's dictionary.

+Caution+.—Use *an, a,* or *the* before each of two or more connected nouns denoting things that are to be distinguished from each other or emphasized.

+Direction+.—*Study the Caution, and correct these errors*:—

1. There is a difference between the sin and sinner. 2. We criticise not the dress but address of the speaker. 3. A noun and pronoun are alike in office. 4. Distinguish carefully between an adjective and adverb. 5. The lion, as well as tiger, belongs to the cat tribe. 6. Neither the North Pole nor South Pole has yet been reached. 7. The secretary and treasurer were both absent.

(*The secretary and treasurer was absent*—referring to one person—is correct.)

+Caution+.—*A few* and *a little* mean *some* as opposed to *none*; *few* means *not many*, and *little* means *not much*.

+Examples+.—He saved *a few* things and *a little* money from the wreck. *Few* shall part where many meet. *Little* was said or done about it.

+Direction+.—*Study the Caution, and correct these errors*:—

1. There are a few pleasant days in March, because it is a stormy month. 2. He saved a little from the fire, as it broke out in the night. 3. Few men live to be & hundred years old, but not many. 4. Little can be done, but not much.

+Direction+.—*Write correct sentences illustrating every point in these Cautions.*

* * * * *

LESSON 91.

CONSTRUCTION OF ADJECTIVES—CONTINUED.

+Caution+.—Choose apt adjectives, but do not use them needlessly; avoid such as repeat the idea or exaggerate it.

+Remark+.—The following adjectives are obviously needless: *Good* virtues, *verdant* green, *painful* toothache, *umbrageous* shade.

+Direction+.—*Study the Caution carefully, and correct these errors*:—

1. It was splendid fun. 2. It was a tremendous dew. 3. He used less words than the other speaker. 4. The lad was neither docile nor teachable. 5. The belief in immortality is common and universal. 6. It was a gorgeous apple. 7. The arm-chair was roomy and capacious. 8. It was a lovely bun, but I paid a frightful price for it.

+Caution+.—So place adjectives that there can be no doubt as to what you intend them to modify. If those forming a series are of different rank, place nearest the noun the one most closely modifying it. If they are of the same rank, place them where they will sound best—generally in the order of length, the shortest first.

+Direction+.—*Study the Caution, and correct these errors:—*

1. A new bottle of wine. 2. The house was comfortable and large. 3. A salt barrel of pork. 4. It was a blue soft beautiful sky. 5. A fried dish of bacon. 6. We saw in the distance a precipitous, barren, towering mountain. 7. Two gray fiery little eyes. 8. A docile and mild pupil. 9. A pupil, docile and mild.

+Direction+.—*Write correct sentences illustrating every point in these two Cautions.*

Miscellaneous Errors.

+Direction+.—*Give the Cautions which these expressions violate, and correct the errors:—*

1. I can bear the heat of summer, but not cold of winter. 2. The North and South Pole. 3. The eldest son of a duke is called *a marquis*. 4. He had deceived me, and so I had a little faith in him. 5. An old and young man. 6. A prodigious snowball hit my cheek. 7. The evil is intolerable and not to be borne. 8. The fat, two lazy men. 9. His penmanship is fearful. 10. A white and red flag were flying. 11. His unusual, unexpected, and extraordinary success surprised him. 12. He wanted a apple, an hard apple. 13. A dried box of herrings. 14. He received a honor. 15. Such an use! 16. The day was delightful and warm. 17. Samuel Adams's habits were unostentatious, frugal, and simple. 18. The victory was complete, though a few of the enemy were killed or captured. 19. The truth is mighty and will prevail. 20. The scepter, the miter, and coronet seem to me poor things for great men to contend for. 21. A few can swim across the Straits of Dover, for the width is great and the current strong. 22. I have a contemptible opinion of you. 23. She has less friends than I.